Personality Theories Workbook

Second Edition

Donna M. Ashcraft
Clarion University of Pennsylvania

THOMSON
~~~~~~*~~~~~~
WADSWORTH

Australia • Canada • Mexico • Singapore • Spain
United Kingdom • United States

THOMSON

WADSWORTH

Editor: *Marianne Taflinger*
Assistant Editor: *Dan Moneypenny*
Editorial Assistant: *Nicole Root*
Marketing Manager: *Kathleen Morgan*
Marketing Assistant: *Laurel Anderson*
Advertising Project Manager: *Samantha Cabaluna*
Project Manager,
   Editorial Production: *Stephanie Zunich*
Print/Media Buyer: *Nancy Panziera*

Permissions Editor: *Connie Dowcett*
Production Service: *Buuji, Inc.*
Text Designer: *Jeanne Calabrese*
Copy Editor: *Robin Gold*
Cover Designer: *Laurie Albrecht*
Compositor: *Buuji, Inc.*
Printer: *Webcom Limited*

Printed in Canada
  2 3 4 5 6 7 06 05 04 03 02

For more information about our products,
contact us at:
Thomson Learning Academic Resource Center
1-800-423-0563

For permission to use material from this text,
contact us by: **Phone:** 1-800-730-2214
Fax: 1-800-730-2215
Web: http://www.thomsonrights.com

ISBN 0-15-505068-0

Wadsworth/Thomson Learning
10 Davis Drive
Belmont, CA 94002-3098
USA

Asia
Thomson Learning
5 Shenton Way #01-01
UIC Building
Singapore 068808

Australia
Nelson Thomson Learning
102 Dodds Street
South Melbourne, Victoria 3205
Australia

Canada
Nelson Thomson Learning
1120 Birchmount Road
Toronto, Ontario M1K 5G4
Canada

Europe/Middle East/Africa
Thomson Learning
High Holborn House
50/51 Bedford Row
London WC1 4LR
United Kingdom

Latin America
Thomson Learning
Seneca, 53
Colonia Polanco
11560 Mexico D.F.
Mexico

Spain
Paraninfo Thomson Learning
Calle/Magallanes, 25
28015 Madrid, Spain

To Paul, Sam, Morgan, and Ryan, again

Preface

Why This Book?

I wrote the first edition of this *Personality Theories Workbook* to provide a resource for instructors of personality courses. As many reviewers of both the first and second editions of this workbook note, many personality theories instructors want to use case studies, but they have been hampered in their efforts because such cases were not readily available. Although many instructors develop their own cases for use in their own courses to demonstrate various concepts, they are limited in the number they can develop because these cases are so time-consuming to develop. This also reflects my experience. While teaching my personality course, I wanted and needed case studies to demonstrate various concepts but could not find them. I therefore started developing my own cases. It seemed silly for everyone who was teaching a course in personality to be reinventing the wheel, so I decided to develop this workbook. Harcourt College Publishers (now Wadsworth Publishing Company) thought it was a good idea and published the first edition. Wadsworth also thought it was a good idea and asked me to write the second edition, improving on the first. I believe that, as fellow instructors, we should all share various resources to make our teaching easier and more effective, and that is what this workbook is about.

More important, I developed this workbook to allow students an opportunity to better learn personality theories and to better understand them by practicing applying the concepts they learned in class or from their texts to behaviors and experiences that could be found in real life. The examples of behaviors and personalities that were found in the case studies in the first edition, and likewise in this second edition do not, for the most part, reflect abnormal behavior but, rather, normal behavior. I wrote them in this way for two basic reasons: (1) They reflect my academic background, which is that of a social/personality psychologist, rather than a clinician. (2) I believe that students should understand that these theories are attempts to explain personality in both the normal and abnormal populations. Because many academicians who teach personality courses are also clinicians, the case studies that they develop and present to their classes reflect that perspective. These are certainly relevant and meaningful, especially considering the number of psychology students who go on to treat clients, but most personality theories were developed to explain behavior more generally. I believe that students need to understand this.

Ethnic and Racial Background Information

This second edition has improved upon the first in a number of ways. First, in response to a number of reviewers, I have given greater attention to ethnic and racial background. Even though the characters in the cases in the first edition varied in experiences, gender, educational levels, sexual orientation, religious affiliation, and socioeconomic status, I avoided references to ethnic or cultural groups in an effort to avoid offending anyone. However, again because so many clinicians teach personality courses, information on these factors is relevant for discussing its implications for therapy. I have therefore included information on ethnic or cultural affiliation in most cases, and I have changed the names of the characters to further reflect this diversity.

Theory Comparison Allowed as Students Progress

Second, although the first edition included cases in the second section that encouraged theory comparison, the second edition allows additional comparison by including questions after each case that directly ask students to compare and contrast theoretical concepts; the second section is still included. The comparison questions in the first section of the workbook are more specific and help students learn individual theoretical concepts by comparing them with similar concepts from other theories and contrasting them with similar concepts so students can see the differences. The cases in the second section encourage more general theory comparison, yet still demonstrate that the same behavior can be explained in several ways by changing focus. A number of application questions have been revised for greater clarification and should benefit student learning as well.

Evolutionary Psychology Concepts Introduced

Finally, I have included two new cases that demonstrate evolutionary psychology concepts, thus expanding the number of cases in the first section to 28 and increasing the number of theories covered in the workbook (and potentially learned by students!) to 14. Additional perspectives give students a broader view of the field of personality.

Acknowledgments

I must express my gratitude to those who helped me to revise this workbook into a second edition. Thanks go to Paul Ashcraft for his support this second time around and for his creative inspiration, editorial assistance, and computer consultation in the first edition. Without him, the first edition would not have been completed, so neither would this second edition. Thanks also to Paul, Sam, Morgan, and Ryan for giving me the time to write the first workbook and revise it this time around. I also appreciate the editorial assistance of Brad Potthoff and Sarah Zedler of Harcourt Brace; Marianne Taflinger of Wadsworth Publishing, and the reviews and suggestions of Beverly Goodwin of Indiana University of Pennsylvania, Claudia Haterkamp of Millersville University of Pennsylvania, Rebekah Bradley of Southern Illinois University—Carbondale, Mike Jordan of Francis Marion University, and Rhonda Mayes of Bowling Green State University in this latest revision.

Contents

SECTION 1
Learning and Applying the Theories   1

SECTION 2
Additional Theory Comparison: Multiple Explanations for the Same Behavior 83

SECTION 1
Learning and Applying the Theories

Freud

Case Study 1

It is Friday night. Hank is sitting in his apartment eating a pint of Ben and Jerry's Cherry Garcia ice cream and contemplating this past week, which had been stressful. He had been considering seeing a therapist about his weight and today saw the therapist for the first time. Hank is five feet six inches tall and weighs 250 pounds. He began thinking about seeing a therapist after yet another woman decided not to continue a relationship with him. After just two dates, Sally told Hank they should not see each other anymore because they were incompatible.

Sally and Hank had met through a chat room espousing the virtues of Macs over PCs, and Hank became impressed with Sally's knowledge of computers and software. After chatting a few times on the computer, Sally and Hank found that they lived in the same city and both were single. Because they seemed to have their love of computers in common, they both thought it would be nice to get to know each other better. They had met for drinks at a mutually agreed upon bar and then went on to dinner. The date did not go as well as Sally had hoped, and one could understand Sally's view. She tends to be a calm, friendly person with an aversion to conflict. Hank, however, tends to be quite sarcastic and often says things to others that offend them. For example, Hank made an unkind comment about Sally's occupation. She is an insurance saleswoman and he implied that she tries to rip off other people by feasting on their insecurities and selling them insurance they do not need. Other examples of his verbal insensitivity include Hank berating the waiter at the restaurant because he was dissatisfied with the service. Hank became so loud that everyone at the restaurant stopped talking to watch Hank and Sally. Sally was mortified.

Far from being occasional, these verbal outbursts seemed to be the norm because Hank engaged in similar behavior on their second date when they went to a computer show. Hank got into an argument with one of the exhibitors about which graphics software package was better.

Unfortunately, Hank has always been sarcastic and his biting comments alienated him from his peers, even as a child. Even when he was growing up, he had difficulty establishing relationships. Friendships were practically nonexistent for

Hank. As a child, while all the other kids were hanging out with their best friends and interacting in groups, Hank was learning to use the computer, which now places him at an advantage in his line of work.

Hank has other annoying habits that tend to alienate others, including Sally. For example, he often chews his fingernails when he is nervous. Although minor, this tendency repulsed Sally. Similarly, he is a chain smoker, and Sally is a nonsmoker.

Hank, however, thought that Sally broke up with him because of his weight problem and soothed his ego by telling himself that she was a very shallow person indeed if she could not see past his appearance and value his personality. After all, his weight was probably partly genetic: his whole family was somewhat over-weight, including his father, mother, and siblings. He also suggested to others (and to himself) that *he* was about to break up with *her*.

The week after his break up with Sally, Hank started experiencing chest pains. After a trip to the emergency room, Hank found out that he had a heart problem. The doctor told him that he must stop smoking, lose weight, change his eating habits, and start an exercise program. Otherwise, he was headed for a heart attack that he might not survive. This was certainly good advice. Hank continuously had something in his mouth, either food or cigarettes. He especially ate and smoked a lot when he was anxious. This news was especially disturbing to Hank, who is rel-atively young. He is a Caucasian man, only 33 years old.

And so Hank was scared into considering seeing a therapist to help him lose weight to improve his health. During his first visit to the therapist, the therapist described himself as psychodynamically oriented and then continued to describe the types of experiences that would occur in the therapy process. Hank felt confi-dence in his therapist by the end of the session and decided to continue so he would lose weight and become healthier.

Hank also thought about the trying week he had at work. As an employee of an advertising firm, Hank primarily worked with computers. He was the person others went to when they had a computer or software question. A whiz at computer graphics, Hank designed and maintains the firm's Web page. Occasionally, he met with clients or potential clients, but his boss usually assigned this duty to other members of the firm. This week, however, his boss asked Hank to meet with a potential client, primarily because the people who usually did so were too busy working to meet a deadline on a different advertising campaign and because other members of the firm were out with the flu. Apparently, the meeting did not go well because shortly afterward his boss called Hank in and chewed him out, stating that this potential client called Hank a loud-mouthed, belligerent cretin. Hank couldn't figure out where this opinion came from; he thought the meeting went pretty well. Sure, he told the client that their health food products were tasteless and that the portions were too small, but the jerk kept self-righteously promoting weight loss and healthy eating. Someone had to put him in his place, Hank thought.

His mother often described Hank in terms that implied that he was loud even when he was a baby. His cries used to pierce the air, and his mother would often rush to make a bottle for Hank or give him a cookie to regain some peace and quiet, even when she could not understand why he was hungry because he had eaten so recently. She laughs about it now, but it was stressful at the time.

The ice cream started to make Hank feel better, more relaxed, and once he finished off the pint, he pulled out a cigarette and lit it. The first inhale also helped to reduce the tension he was feeling. He hoped that the next week would be better.

Hank wished that his co-workers would appreciate him and offer him friendship. When he was younger, he thought that by becoming good at computers (which he thought were cool), and being able to answer other people's questions about computers, he would be able to make contact with others and form the close relationships that other people do, but so far, this strategy has been unsuccessful. More than anything, Hank wishes a woman would fall in love with him. He thinks that love will solve all his problems: He would not be lonely anymore, and he would be able to lose weight and quit smoking, too, if he just had the love of a woman.

Application Questions

Use Freud's states of consciousness and stages of psychosexual development to help explain Hank's behavior by answering the following questions.

1. What personality (or character) type does Hank display according to Freudian theory? Why do you think so? At what stage is Hank fixated, according to the Freudian perspective? Find evidence of fixation in the case study. What would have caused this fixation?

2. Would Freudian theory describe Hank's eating and argumentative behaviors as being internally or externally motivated? Explain the motivation.

3. Find an example of a Freudian defense mechanism that Hank uses in this description. Explain it.

4. Find an example of regression in the case study. Explain it.

5. Would a Freudian therapist view Hank's weight problem as a behavioral problem in and of itself, or as a symptom of another problem? Explain.

6. What therapeutic techniques would a Freudian therapist, like the one in the case study, likely use? What state of consciousness would be the focus of therapy? What brings healing in Freudian therapy?

Theory Comparison Questions

1. Use another theory, besides Freud's, to explain Hank's eating and argumentative behavior.

2. What aspect of Hank's behavior would be the focus of a therapist who is behaviorally oriented? What aspect would be the focus if the therapist were psychodynamically oriented?

3. Use Erikson's concept of lack of intimacy to explain Hank's problems in establishing long-term relationships with women. How does this differ from the Freudian explanation?

Freud

Case Study 2

Steve is sitting at a restaurant table waiting for his date to come back from the bathroom. As he waits, he imagines what the rest of the evening will be like. The restaurant they are eating at is one of those little Italian places with red-and-white checkered tablecloths and candles in Chianti bottles. A violin player paces around the tables while he plays romantic music. Steve contemplates that these types of restaurants always work well for him. His date would be charmed by the atmosphere and begin to feel romantic. This would allow Steve to make his move, and typically, he and his date would end up at either his apartment or hers for a night of passion.

Steve is 38, of Italian-American descent, and single: a bachelor by choice, but his friends worry about his happiness. They wonder if Steve is unable to form a long-term relationship, that he has a fear of commitment and an addiction to sex and the passion that marks the beginning of relationships. And, they wonder whether Steve's strained relationship with his mother is at least partly to blame for his behavior. Steve's mother, while caring for his physical needs, was not openly affectionate and did not give Steve the physical affection and loving interaction he craved. They wonder if his anger toward her and her negligent behavior toward Steve is being manifested as anger toward women in general.

Steve has been a flirt ever since puberty. In high school, he had a reputation for his insincerity. Girls were attracted to him; he was handsome and spent a lot of time and money on his appearance. Unbeknownst to his friends, however, Steve secretly feared that he was unattractive, so he did whatever he could to improve his looks.

The girls he asked out always had a good time on their dates, but it soon became known that he would always pressure his dates for sex, and, in many cases, tell them that he loved them to convince them to have sex. He was also rumored to have made one girl pregnant and then claimed that it was not his child. To his close male friends, he said that she was not going to tie him down, that "there were too many women and not enough time."

This pattern of relationships continued during college. He would date women, have sex with them a few times, and then break off the relationship. He estimated that by the time he was 21, he had had sex with about eight dozen women. He bragged about this among his male friends.

After college, and through the present time, Steve also continued to form relationships with women that were based on sexual attraction and nothing more substantial. One by one, he watched his male friends settle down and commit to one woman. Every time this happened, he would express astonishment and disbelief, stating that his friends were being duped and that no one would make him live with one woman for the rest of his life. When women agreed to go out with him or go to bed with him, Steve felt attractive and no one was going to take that away from him. In fact, Steve secretly feared that no woman would find him attractive enough to marry. He believed that these women went out with him initially to get a free meal and would soon want to break up with him when someone better came around. So he broke up with them first.

His friends had believed that Steve's latest conquest, Diane, would be the one he would marry. She seemed to be all that any man could hope for. She was pretty, smart, and caring and had a good sense of humor. Steve had been dating her for longer than he normally dated women, and his friends thought that he was finally growing up and settling down. As it turns out, the relationship lasted longer than usual because she was reluctant to have sex with him. She finally did after a couple of months when she was convinced that Steve really loved her and was not just using her for sex. Unfortunately, Diane should have trusted her initial instincts. Steve broke up with her after they had sex on three different occasions.

His present date was a woman he met at the gym he worked out at. She was very attractive, with a great body. He used to date women he met at work, but after someone accused him of sexual harassment, he decided to no longer date women from work. He was angered by the specific accusation and the hype associated with sexual harassment in general. A man just couldn't follow his instincts any more without the possibility of losing his job. At least he could still meet women at other places.

Application Questions

Use Freud's states of consciousness and stages of psychosexual development to help explain Steve's behavior by answering the following questions.

1. Does the Freudian perspective indicate that Steve's relationships with women are internally or externally motivated? Which system of personality is most involved? How?

2. According to Freudian theory, is Steve aware of why he interacts with women on only a sexual basis? Which state of consciousness is most involved in controlling this behavior?

3. What type of Freudian psychic energy motivates Steve's relationships with women?

4. Which of Freud's personality types does Steve display? What evidence is there for it? What would have caused it?

5. At what Freudian stage is Steve fixated? What evidence is there of it? Describe the stage and how it contributed to the fixation. What would have caused this fixation?

6. Others might express their behavior differently than Steve if they were fixated at the same stage. Give some examples of how they might behave.

Theory Comparison Questions

1. How could Fromm's relatedness need explain Steve's relationships with women? How does this compare with the Freudian explanation?

2. How could Horney's concept of basic anxiety explain Steve's relationships with women?

3. How does Melanie Klein's conceptualization of the Oedipus complex differ from that of Freud? Do these distinctions make a difference in explaining Steve's relationships with women? If so, how?

Jung

Case Study 3

For lack of a better term, we can describe Bob as a fortuneteller of sorts, a mystic. He is 56, with an Irish American ancestry and accent, and earns his living by telling people what they can expect to happen in the future. This is accomplished by reading tarot cards and by laying his hands on his clients. He claims to "sense" things when he does this; he can see what will happen to his client. He does not understand how it happens, but he can almost see things in his mind's eye.

He also earns money by contacting people who "have crossed over to the other world." In other words, he claims to be able to talk with the dead. To do this, he must be able to have contact with an article that the deceased touched. Bob explains that it is not the feel of the object that is important in this feat or in predicting the future; rather, it is being able to experience a person's (dead or alive) "psychic energy." After touching the object, he then concentrates and goes into a type of trance in which he makes contact with, and talks to, the deceased. His clients believe he is actually doing this. They claim that he tells them things only their deceased loved ones would know.

Bob has always had these types of abilities. As a teenager, he would frequently sense that a particular event would occur, or he would know that something had happened even though no one had told him. These were both minor, and more major, experiences. For example, when he was younger, Bob would know when to put the coffee on for his father who worked irregular hours. Bob just knew when his father was coming home, and his father always wanted a cup of coffee when he got home. Likewise, when his grandfather died, Bob was filled with a sense of foreboding. Only later that day did Bob learn about the death and why he felt this sense of dread.

Even though Bob has always had these psychic experiences, he hasn't always been as interested in the paranormal as he is today. This interest, though always present, really did not expand and encompass his life until he reached the age of 40. As he neared his 40th birthday, Bob contemplated death and began to study paranormal activities. This study increased his understanding of his own experiences and allowed him to hone his mystical skills, which in turn, gradually led to his current occupation and lifestyle.

Today, Bob earns money speaking to groups of interested parties about the paranormal. At these events, he describes his experiences and his beliefs about the "other world." He especially enjoys this type of interaction. It makes him feel knowledgeable and sage, as though he were a prophet and the members of his audience were his disciples. His last speaking engagement drew a crowd of 2500 at a college in California. During this "performance," he singled out a number of people and spoke to them directly, giving them messages from deceased loved ones. Stopping in the middle of his talk, he pointed to one young woman in the audience and told her that her father had a message for her, that he "understands and forgives." She broke down in tears. He told another woman that her deceased husband wanted to let her know that he was all right and happy.

His friends describe Bob as impractical. Although he has been able to make a living this way, Bob has trouble with everyday tasks: keeping house, keeping track of his money, having enough food. His house is always messy; he needs an accountant to keep track of his money; and he often goes to the refrigerator or cupboard, only to find nothing substantial to eat.

His household is decidedly different from most people's. Certainly, it resembles more of the life of a rock star than the life of a banker, with all his traveling and his "performances." Even when he is at home for an extended period, however, he has many more visitors than most people have because of people who make appointments with him for "advice" and guidance. These sessions are when he uses his mystical tools and powers to give his clients information from "the other side."

His friends consider him somewhat odd and eccentric, not surprisingly. Other people who do not know Bob very well think that he is either wacko or a con artist. Even his agent/manager thinks of him as only entertainment. Although Bob occasionally is concerned that he is "selling out," he believes that he is helping others.

Application Questions

Using Jung's theoretical concepts and stages, assess Bob's personality by answering the following questions.

1. What is Bob's attitude according to Jungian theory? Why do you believe so?

2. What is Bob's superior function according to Jungian theory? Why do you believe so?

3. What are archetypes? In what level of consciousness are they contained, according to Jung's theory? What archetype has Bob been influenced by? How do you know this? How does it influence his behavior?

4. At what stage is Bob presently, according to Jungian theory? What types of events should he be experiencing at this stage? Is there evidence for these experiences in the case study?

Theory Comparison Questions

1. At what stage of development would Erikson place Bob? Why? How do Erikson's psychosocial stages differ from Jung's stages of development?

2. How could Fromm's concept of the existential dilemmas explain Bob's experiences with mysticism? Compare this concept with Jung's archetypes.

Jung

Case Study 4

Mark is a 28-year-old, African-American firefighter who loves his job. Although it does not pay as well as he would like and the hours are irregular, it is a rewarding and thrilling occupation. As he attempts to describe why he likes his job so much, his face transforms. It lights up. He looks as if he is reliving the excitement of the latest event that his fire company had been called to. He explains that when the alarm sounds, adrenaline rushes into his system and his body springs to life. He states that when he is on a call, he does not actually feel fear, but rather feels caution—and he feels alive. When he sees the brightness of the fire and feels the heat from the flames, he functions almost automatically, performing his duties bravely, but not carelessly. The sight and feel of the blaze and the rawness of his lungs from occasionally breathing in smoke make him aware of his mortality and make him appreciate life.

Part of Mark's job also consists of giving talks to elementary school children about fire hazards and fire safety. He discusses how fires start and grow. He discusses what children should do if a fire breaks out. When he gives these talks the children look up to him and see him as brave, which makes him feel good. He also enjoys the status associated with being a firefighter. The people he helps reward him with praise and thanks. They, like the school children, make him feel important and valiant.

Mark's job is very stimulating. Even as a child, Mark was always seeking out high levels of stimulation. When he was very young, he was always making noise. Either he was continuously talking or singing or he was trying to make music with such things like sticks and pots and pans. Sometimes he would claim that it "was just too quiet." Favorite games were exciting also. Frequently, he would play games in which he was some kind of super hero. He would be the sheriff who captured the bank robbers; the police officer who threw the bad guys in jail; the captain who outwitted the pirates (and often it was his little sister who was the bad guy or the pirate or the bank robber).

As a teenager and young adult, he always knew he would go into some type of "service" occupation like fire fighting or police duty, and he actually attended the police academy for a short time before deciding that it was not for him. He was concerned that the job would turn out to be monotonous rather than stimulating because of the amount of paperwork to do and the continuous driving involved in patrols. After his experience with police work, Mark decided on becoming a fire-fighter because he found it more exciting. This decision was a difficult one for him because his parents disapproved of his career choice. They were concerned about Mark getting hurt or killed. They also disliked the idea of him moving out of their house to go to the fire-training academy. Nevertheless, he made his decision and stayed with it. He performed very well at the academy and rented his own apartment for the times he would not be living at the fire station.

Mark's friends describe him as outgoing, and happy. He loves life and lives it to its fullest. Although he isn't an introspective person, he is very realistic and pragmatic. His fire-fighting colleagues describe him as very competent, always able to adapt rescue techniques to the situation as necessary. He is even quite good at fixing and making things. He has renovated the kitchen of the fire-house recently and enjoyed doing so in his free time. He likes the feel of working with tools and the smell of newly cut wood.

Application Questions

Using Jung's theoretical concepts and stages, assess Mark's personality by answering the following questions.

1. What is Mark's attitude according to Jungian theory? Why do you believe so?

2. What is Mark's superior function according to Jungian theory? Why do you believe so?

3. According to Jung's theory, what archetype has Mark been influenced by? How do you know this? How does it influence his behavior? Is Mark aware of its influence? Why?

4. At what stage is Mark presently, according to Jung's theory? Specify sub-stage, if appropriate. What types of events should be occurring at this stage?

5. At what stage, in Jungian theory, was Mark when he was pretending to be a super hero? Specify sub-stage if appropriate.

Theory Comparison Questions

1. Use another theory, besides Jung's, to explain Mark's career choice.

2. How could behaviorism explain Mark's career choice? What are some reinforcements that encourage this behavior? How is the focus of behaviorism different than that of Jung's theory in explaining Mark's career choice?

3. How could Eysenck's concept of extraversion explain Mark's career choice? What other behaviors could this concept explain?

Erikson

Case Study 5

Chrystell is a happy 8-year-old who is just finishing the third grade. Like all parents, Chrystell's were worried about how she would react and be reacted to in school. They were especially concerned because they and Chrystell are of African-American heritage and Chrystell would be attending a primarily Caucasian school. They need not have worried. She is doing well. The other children like her and she has made many friends. Likewise, she does well scholastically. Not only does she fulfill the curriculum objectives, she surpasses them. For example, Chrystell began learning to read in kindergarten, an activity that usually does not begin until the first grade. Part of the reason that Chrystell does so well in school is because Chrystell's parents are quick to praise her scholastic efforts and help her with schoolwork if she has trouble.

It seems as though Chrystell has always been easy to take care of. As a baby, her mother had nursed Chrystell on demand and found that she really did not demand it that often. In fact, there were many times that her mother offered the child the breast because she felt it had been too long since Chrystell had last eaten. Even after waking up in the morning, Chrystell did not cry hysterically for food. Her mother really did not even feel as exhausted by the newborn as she had been with her other children because she was able to get six hours of sleep starting fairly soon after Chrystell was born. Nighttime feedings came only once and they were quick; her mother was even able to fall asleep while Chrystell was feeding and then when she woke up, she would put Chrystell back in the crib, return to her own bed, and fall asleep again herself.

Potty training was not terribly stressful either. Neither Chrystell's mother or her father felt that they should rush their children into being potty-trained. They believed the kids would eventually learn control and that it was the parent's role to introduce the idea of using the potty to the children and to encourage them, but not force them, into using it if they were not ready. Chrystell's parent's tried not to embarrass her when she had accidents; instead, they reminded her to try to remember to use the potty the next time. This approach worked for Chrystell: She learned to use the potty when she was about 2 1/2 years old without much hassle.

Chrystell's parents took this approach for helping her, and their other children, to reach other milestones as well. They encouraged their children to do things like walk, hold a spoon, and feed themselves. They tried to make those activities easier to learn for their children by practicing the activities with them, showing them how to do something, and, sometimes, buying things like curved spoons, which made it easier to learn to get the spoon to the mouth without dumping its contents. Chrystell's parents tried not to hurry their children into learning these activities, although sometimes it was difficult not to. Most of the time, if an activity seemed too difficult they would forget about it for a short while and try it with Chrystell or her siblings again later.

As Chrystell got older, her parents tried not to dictate which activities she should play. Instead, they gave her a couple of choices and let her choose which she preferred. Many times her parents did not need to even do this because often Chrystell would just go off on her own and amuse herself. Sometimes she would just look at pictures in books. At other times, she would play with her dolls. At still other times, she would play with her Legos®.

The only time Chrystell's parents could remember having trouble with her was when her little sister was born. Chrystell's younger sister was a demanding baby and had been born through Caesarean section, so her mother had been limited physically in what she could do with Chrystell and in the time she could spend with her. Chrystell tried to express affection toward the baby but sometimes would hug her too hard. Chrystell's mother was not sure whether this was done on purpose or not. She thought that Chrystell was jealous of the baby because she would say things like, "You always hold the baby, Mommy." Chrystell also started to stutter. Chrystell's Mom would try to reassure her by saying things like, "I know you feel like the baby gets more attention than you but I held you this much when you were a baby too." Her mom tried to be understanding of Chrystell's jealousy and did not try to make Chrystell feel bad about it. When her mother was finally feeling better, the baby was less demanding, and her mother was able to spend more time with Chrystell, the stuttering eventually went away and Chrystell became gentler with the baby.

Now as this school year ends, Chrystell's mother hopes that the rest of her school experiences go just as well and that her influence will continue to guide Chrystell's development positively.

Application Questions

Using Erikson's psychosocial stages of development (especially the first through the fourth) analyze Chrystell's life by answering the following questions.

1. What is the crisis experienced in Erikson's first stage of psychosocial development? How did Chrystell resolve this stage? What was the outcome of the crisis? Was it favorable or unfavorable?

2. What is the crisis experienced in Erikson's second stage of psychosocial development? How did Chrystell resolve this stage? What was the outcome of the crisis? Was it favorable or unfavorable?

3. What is the crisis experienced in Erikson's third stage of psychosocial development? How did Chrystell resolve this stage? What was the outcome of the crisis? Was it favorable or unfavorable?

4. What is the crisis experienced in Erikson's fourth stage of psychosocial development? How did Chrystell resolve this stage? What was the outcome of the crisis? Was it favorable or unfavorable?

5. Erikson's theory is sometimes described as a good guide for parents. Find examples of this guidance in the case study and describe them.

Theory Comparison Questions

1. How could Maslow's theory explain Chrystell's experiences? Are all her needs fulfilled? Explain. How do Maslow's needs compare with Erikson's stage crises?

2. Use Bandura's concept of reciprocal determinism to explain how Chrystell's stuttering was resolved after her baby sister was born. How is Bandura's theory different from Erikson's in its emphasis?

3. How could Sullivan's good mother/bad mother personification explain Chrystell's breastfeeding experiences? How is the emphasis of Sullivan's theory similar to that of Erikson's?

Erikson

Case Study 6

Betty, Caucasian and now 68, contemplates her life. She sent her children off to college and eventually saw them fall in love, get married, and start families of their own. She should be happy, but she is not. Instead, she feels dissatisfied and wonders if her life would be better if she divorced her husband of more than 40 years. She would like to do so but lacks the confidence to carry out this drastic change. She doesn't believe she could live on her own. She always had someone to take care of her: first her parents, then her husband. Now she doesn't believe that she could support herself financially.

Betty's childhood was fairly uneventful. She was the second of two children; her brother is three years older than she is. Her parents were both of above-average intelligence, and her family could be considered middle class. Although she grew up in the 1930s, she was probably less affected by the Great Depression than were most because her father's job had survived so he was able to keep food on the table. Although they were certainly not rich, they at least had the necessities, which is more than many families had then. She lived a fairly sheltered childhood but attended school and made a few friends there. She was an average student, getting mostly Bs and Cs for grades. Although similar to those of her friends, her parents were disappointed with her grades and let her know about that. They believed she should be doing better because they had done better in school and because her older brother did much better; he was an exceptional student.

Betty's main ambition was to get married and have a family. This was a typical ambition for girls at that time. In the 1940s and 1950s, middle-class girls found a husband by attending college, which she did. Betty attended an all-girl college and majored in education, one of the acceptable majors for young women then. However, she dated infrequently probably because (1) she felt that the other women in her classes were wittier and more attractive (she often referred to herself as a Plain Jane, both in outward appearance and in personality) and because (2) her father often forbade her to attend social functions held by the close-by, all-male academy, even though they were extremely well chaperoned. Despite these obstacles, Betty met and dated one man in college with whom she fell in love. Unfortunately, this young man did not return her feelings.

Betty earned her teaching degree and then taught for several years. While attending another college one summer to take additional education courses, she met a young man, Cole, who was also attending college. They dated, and after the summer, they continued a long distance relationship by writing letters to each other. After six months, Cole proposed to her in a letter. She accepted. She was 26 at the time and he was 28. In the 1950s, a woman who was 26 was considered "over the hill," with little chance of getting married. This was probably one reason she accepted his proposal. She saw it as her last opportunity for marriage. Betty's parents disapproved of the match but eventually came to accept it.

Betty gave up her teaching career, as was the practice at the time, to become a wife and eventually a mother. Unfortunately for Betty, married life was not what she expected. Cole was employed by a business that required him to do a lot of traveling. Likewise, his job forced him, and his family, to move frequently. Eventually Betty became dissatisfied with moving every two to three years. She wanted roots and children and she thought that it was important that their children develop long-term friendships. After being married for five years, Betty and Cole had their first child, a son. Two years later Betty had a miscarriage and two years after that, a second son. Over time, Betty became more devoted to her children than to her husband. For example, her first child was allowed to be read four books and sing four songs before bedtime, but she granted her husband very little of her attention. The attention he did receive was often in the form of criticism.

After 15 years of marriage, Betty had had enough moving around and the family bought a house in Connecticut. Her husband was able to obtain a position in his employer's New York City branch, and he commuted home on weekends. Having only a weekend husband and father certainly took its toll on Betty and Cole's marriage, but Betty continued to raise her two sons and attend her children's extracurricular activities. She also became an active member of her church where she taught Sunday school and organized the church social hour.

Now that her children are grown and have families of their own, Betty wonders why she should continue to live with a man she feels so distant from and how she could begin to feel needed again. She wishes she could relocate closer to one of her children, but they have families of their own and she does not want to intrude.

Application Questions

Using Erikson's psychosocial stages of development (especially the fourth through the eighth), analyze Betty's life by answering the following questions.

1. Would Eriksonian theory suggest that Betty's behavior is internally or externally motivated? What motivates it? Which system of personality is most involved in personality, according to the theory?

2. What is the crisis experienced in Erikson's fourth stage of psychosocial development? How did Betty resolve this stage? What was the outcome of the crisis? Was it favorable or unfavorable?

3. What is the crisis experienced in Erikson's fifth stage of psychosocial development? How did Betty resolve this stage? What was the outcome of the crisis? Was it favorable or unfavorable?

4. What is the crisis experienced in Erikson's sixth stage of psychosocial development? How did Betty resolve this stage? What was the outcome of the crisis? Was it favorable or unfavorable?

5. What is the crisis experienced in Erikson's seventh stage of psychosocial development? How did Betty resolve this stage? What was the outcome of the crisis? Was it favorable or unfavorable?

6. What could be expected in the eighth stage of Betty's life according to Erikson's theory?

Theory Comparison Questions

1. Which of Fromm's needs have been met for Betty? Which have not? Explain. How does Fromm's theory compare with Erikson's in their consideration of social influence?

2. How would Rogers's concept of conditions of worth explain Betty's career choice? Her marriage to Cole? How is the emphasis of Rogers's theory different than that of Erikson's?

3. At what Jungian stage could Betty be placed? Why? How do Jung's stages compare with those of Erikson?

Adler

Case Study 7

Martin is extremely successful by almost anyone's standards. He is a criminal lawyer who earns approximately a half million dollars each year defending rich, and sometimes well-known, clients against criminal charges ranging from drunk driving and marijuana possession to murder. His salary allows him a life of luxury. He owns two houses, one worth a million dollars in Connecticut, from which he commutes to New York City to do most of his work and a "cabin" in the mountains of Colorado where he vacations often and that is worth about a half million dollars. He owns a Jaguar convertible (racing green), a Lexus, and a Range Rover. He buys designer clothes and eats at all the best restaurants. He attends the theater and art openings.

Martin's life has not always been luxurious, however. He actually came from very humble beginnings. He was born in a medium-sized city in a very Polish-American neighborhood. His parents were working class, and neither parent finished high school. His mother stayed home with the children. Although his father was a carpenter by trade, he sometimes had trouble finding work because of discriminatory practices. Others did not want to hire him because they distrusted members of his ethnic group. At times, the family was eligible for welfare assistance, but his father refused to apply for it because it would have hurt his pride. Occasionally, the children went to bed hungry because of this.

Martin's mother was from a family that had more money than her husband's family did. She had gotten pregnant by Martin's father when she was just 19. Although her parents did not approve of the match, believing that she was marrying below her status, they forced Martin's mother into the marriage because of the pregnancy. Martin was the product of that pregnancy. After Martin's birth, it became very clear to his mother that she preferred the more privileged life she had lived when she was single. Eventually, this realization made her resent both Martin and his father. Being staunch Catholics, however, they never considered divorce, and the couple had two more children.

Neither parent was very affectionate toward the children, and sometimes the children's basic physical needs were not even met, especially when Martin's father was out of work. Martin often felt alone and commented at one point that neither of his parents really loved him. Martin felt embarrassed by his humble beginnings. In particular, he was embarrassed by his ethnic background, his parent's lack of education, and his lack of material goods. He became determined to rise above his early station in life and achieve a more successful and sophisticated life.

Martin prefers to not think about or discuss his childhood. On the very rare occasion when he does think about his past, he recalls a very early memory about another child who had been unjustly accused of stealing an item from a store. The item had actually fallen down and rolled under the counter. Martin defended the child and showed the store clerk the dropped item, thus saving an innocent child from being unjustly punished.

Martin was an excellent student in grade school and high school; he earned a full scholarship to the University of Michigan where he graduated with honors; and he attended Harvard Law School. He passed the bar the first time around. Other students and some of his professors commented on Martin's penetrating intellect and his uniform determination to excel in academics. However, they also remarked about how few friendships he had, his lack of female companionship, and his disinterest in any of the other activities on campus that were either of entertainment value or contributed to the well-being of the university.

Martin started at a well-known law firm and was on the fast track toward a partnership, but he became disgruntled with the politics of the firm and the social games being played. He left to start a new firm of his own, and some of his clients went with him. His reputation as a defense lawyer grew quickly, and he soon found his firm and his wallet growing in size.

Because he is well known, several organizations have asked him to be on their boards of directors, but he has refused all of them. Martin is not active in any community activities and does no volunteer work, not even pro bono work.

Application Questions

Using Adler's theory of individual psychology, analyze Martin's life by answering the following questions.

1. What evidence is there that Martin had feelings of inferiority?

2. According to Adlerian theory, how did feelings of inferiority influence Martin's behavior? What influence did these beliefs of inferiority have on his striving for superiority?

3. According to Adler's theory, what was Martin's goal? What was Martin's unique style of life that could be used to achieve this goal? How do you know this?

4. Did Martin have a high or low level of social interest? What does this imply about his personality and adjustment? What is the cause of this level of social interest?

5. What did Adler say about birth order that would apply to Martin's life?

Theory Comparison Questions

1. How could Horney's concept of basic anxiety explain Martin's exaggerated independence? What mechanisms are used by Martin to help him deal with basic anxiety? How does Adler's concept of social interest compare with Horney's trend of moving away from people?

2. How do Adler's safeguarding tendencies compare with Horney's neurotic trends? Explain Martin's lack of relationships using these two concepts.

3. How does Adler's superiority complex compare with Horney's concept of idealized self?

Adler

Case Study 8

Toshimi is a ballet dancer and teacher. She has her own ballet school in Detroit and teaches dozens of children, mostly girls, how to *plié,* the correct positions for their arms and legs, and how to go *en pointe.* Looking at her now, anyone would think that she is the epitome of health. She is thin, with an athletic build, strong yet graceful, and very coordinated. Her school is the best in the city, and a few of her students have gone on to train and dance with prestigious dance companies.

Toshimi was not always athletic or graceful, though. As a child, Toshimi was very sickly, and because of a variety of health problems, she was not able to play physical games like tag and baseball very well with other children. She was born prematurely and almost died a few days later from a respiratory infection. Later in childhood, she developed a severe case of tuberculosis, from which she gradually recovered. As an only child, her parents became overprotective of Toshimi, and for years encouraged her to "take it easy," not run around very much, and not become too excited. Essentially, they encouraged Toshimi to become fragile. Her inactivity left her awkward and out of shape which, in turn, resulted in an ineptitude for childhood games. She felt as though her friends were better than she was, at least in terms of physical activity and, unfortunately, she was right. In fact, one of her earliest memories was of not being chosen to be on anyone's baseball team. The other children chose other friends to be on the two teams but both team captains, although they liked Toshimi, refused to let her on their team because she was too clumsy and slow. Toshimi, feeling very embarrassed, returned home alone. When she returned home, she turned on the television. As she flipped through the channels, a program on PBS caught her eye. She saw women and men in beautiful costumes perform incredible physical feats. The women were able to stand on their toes, and both the men and women were able to perform graceful leaps. As she watched the Swan Lake ballet, Toshimi became determined. Rather than resulting in depression, thinking about this painful experience of not being chosen for a team made Toshimi very determined to become healthy and physically fit. She wanted more than anything to be good at some kind of physical activity and to have others respect her athleticism.

Toshimi nagged her overprotective parents into letting her take ballet lessons. They reluctantly gave in, thinking (incorrectly) that dance was not very strenuous. They loved their daughter and hated to deny her anything. At first, Toshimi was incredibly incompetent and clumsy in dance class, but she had a patient and understanding teacher who discouraged the other children from snickering. Toshimi gradually became stronger and more coordinated. Eventually, she started to show some talent for the ballet, especially for choreography. Her teacher also noted her determination and talent and discussed the possibility of training for a career in dance. After discussion with her parents, Toshimi was allowed to take extra dance classes at a summer camp for dancers, which she did for a number of years. At first, the camp dance teacher was reluctant to take Toshimi as a student because she was older than most of the girls, but was convinced to work with Toshimi for a short time and then determine whether Toshimi should stay on. Soon, it was very clear that Toshimi had talent. She stood out in a performance, and she was a gifted choreographer.

Toshimi's life changed dramatically when she moved to live with the dancers at the camp. She found that her every whim was no longer satisfied and that she had to wait her turn for various things—from brushing her teeth, to getting food, to using the phone to call her parents, to talking and working with her teacher. Although she found it difficult, Toshimi eventually adjusted to this lifestyle, and as she adjusted she found herself caring for some of the other younger girls. She was the oldest and found herself in the role of a big sister. She comforted the younger girls and gave them advice, as they needed it. They looked up to her, especially when they needed comfort. This was quite a change for Toshimi. When she had lived with her parents, it was she who needed comforting, for example, as in the time when no one wanted her on their baseball team. Now her role was reversed.

Although Toshimi showed determination and talent, once her body matured at puberty, it became evident that she did not have the body type necessary for a successful career in dance. Her delay in taking lessons also put her at a disadvantage. Furthermore, because of discriminatory practices, it was very difficult for a woman of Asian descent (or any other minority) to begin a career as a professional dancer when Toshimi was attempting to do so. Although disappointed, Toshimi would not be stopped from pursuing her dream. She continued to take dance lessons, and in college, she majored in dance and minored in business. When she completed her degree, she opened her own dance studio with a loan from her parents and began giving dance lessons to children. Her reputation as an experienced, talented, and patient ballet teacher grew and her enrollment enlarged. Today there is a waiting list to begin lessons at her school. She is also beginning to get a reputation regionally and even nationally because a number of her students have been accepted to train with such prestigious ballet companies as the New York City Ballet and American Ballet Theater.

Application Questions

Using Adler's theory of individual psychology, analyze Toshimi's life by answering the following questions.

    1. What is the motivation behind Toshimi's career choice, according to Adler's theory?

    2. According to Adlerian theory, what was Toshimi's goal? What was Toshimi's unique style of life that could be used to achieve this goal? How do you know this?

    3. Did Toshimi have a high or low level of social interest? What does this imply about her personality and adjustment? What is the cause of this level of social interest?

    4. What did Adler say about birth order that would apply to Toshimi's life?

Theory Comparison Questions

    1. What other theory, besides Adler's, could explain Toshimi's career choice? How?

    2. How do Adler's thoughts on parenting compare with Erikson's? Would Adler consider Toshimi's parents as having good parenting skills? What about Erikson?

Horney

Case Study 9

Samara just cannot understand why she is still single at age 35 when all her friends are happily married. She sees herself as loving, generous, and unselfish. Certainly she is sensitive to the needs of others, much more so than her friends seem to be. Her friends seem to criticize their husbands; she would never do that. Certainly, she would not force her mate into going to see a movie or play that she wanted to see but that he did not.

Getting married is especially important to Samara because she was raised in a very traditional mideastern household where the role of the woman is to be someone's wife and mother. It isn't that she doesn't try to establish relationships. In fact, she has had many relationships with men; they just don't last. For example, her last boyfriend, Tom, broke up with her after six months. He claimed that she was too pushy and possessive. Samara was pushing him to get married, and he was not ready for that kind of commitment yet. He was also concerned about her jealousy. Samara hated it when Tom showed attention to other women—even though the attention was platonic. Tom has a number of women friends and keeps in touch with them by calling them and talking on the telephone. He also goes to lunch with them occasionally. Likewise, Tom has a number of female colleagues at work. Samara often complained to Tom that he spent too much time with other women and not enough time with her. Even though Tom continuously tried to reassure Samara that these relationships with women were nonsexual and that they were friends to him, not potential dates, Samara continued to discourage these relationships. Samara was terrified that Tom would find these other women more attractive and desert her. She just did not want to be alone again.

Actually, Samara is rarely "alone." She goes from a breakup to another relationship very quickly. She had broken up with another boyfriend, Fred, two weeks before she met Tom and they started dating. One month before beginning to date Fred, she experienced another breakup, this time initiated by Paul. The breakup with Paul was fairly vicious, and again, Samara had trouble understanding why it happened. She did her best to make Paul happy. She let him decide where they would go and what they would do on dates. She even let him decide what to order for her at restaurants. When Paul would ask her what she wanted to do, she always replied, "whatever you want." Samara just couldn't understand how men could not appreciate what a giving, unselfish person she was.

She was always there for her current boyfriend. When he was having a difficult time, she would listen to his problems very attentively and help him feel better. She would do this even when she too had a problem she wanted to discuss, but she always put his needs before her own. Instead of appreciating these qualities, the men she dated disliked them. At the time of their breakup, Paul, for example, complained that Samara was too mousy, that he did not know what she liked to do or even eat! He said that he could not get to know her and therefore did not want a relationship with her. He found her submissiveness annoying, not endearing. He also complained, like Tom, about Samara's possessiveness. Paul sometimes wanted to spend time alone or with his male friends, but Samara resented this time away from her. In fact, the week before they broke up, Samara and Paul had a huge argument about Paul's friends. Samara had gone shopping and was in the process of cooking an elaborate meal—Paul's favorite—but Paul called to tell her that he ran into an old buddy who was in town just for the night and that he couldn't see her that evening; he was going to go out with his buddy. Paul had no idea that she was planning to cook a big meal for him; he thought they were planning to go out for a burger at his favorite bar. Samara became angry because of her wasted effort and told him how unappreciative he was. He in turn, complained about her unreasonable assumptions and possessiveness. That argument led to the breakup the following week.

Now, with the breakup with Tom, Samara is again asking friends to fix her up. As she commiserates with her friends, she tells them that all she wants is someone to love her, that if you have love, you have everything. She wonders if she will ever find the right man.

Application Questions

Using Horney's psychoanalytic social theory, analyze Samara's behavior by answering the following questions.

1. Which of Horney's trends (or basic adjustments) is Samara demonstrating? Explain.

2. Which of Horney's neurotic needs does Samara demonstrate? Find examples in the case study.

3. According to Horney's theory, what is the cause of Samara's neurotic behavior?

4. Is Samara's self-image an accurate one? How could Horney's theory explain the discrepancy between Samara's idealized versus real image of herself?

Theory Comparison Questions

1. Is there a discrepancy between Samara's organismic self and her perceived or ideal self? Explain. How do Horney's concepts of idealized and real selves compare with Rogers's concepts of organismic, perceived, and ideal selves?

2. How can Kelly's individuality corollary explain the difference in opinion between Samara and her boyfriends on the status of their relationships?

Horney

Case Study 10

At the age of 23, Shimin has just earned his master's degree in mathematics and is about to begin his first, full-time, permanent position with a General Motors Research Facility. He had other part time jobs to get him through his education, but now he has finally begun his career. One of the part time jobs he had was as an instructor in the department where he was completing his master's degree requirements. This position initially required that Shimin teach three sections of an introductory level math course each semester in return for a tuition waver and a small stipend. However, Shimin did not enjoy the teaching experience, and apparently, his students did not either. Shimin was displeased with his students' lack of enthusiasm. He complained that his students were not really trying to learn and that they were not interested in the material. He frequently found himself comparing himself as a freshman to the students that he was now teaching, and he always found that he compared favorably to his students. He was more interested, more enthusiastic, he worked harder and longer, he was more persistent, and so on. His students complained that Shimin was difficult to understand, that he covered the material too quickly, and that he was unapproachable. They complained that he made them feel stupid when they asked questions, and so they stopped asking questions. Moreover, their grades suffered because of it. These complaints made their way back to the mathematics department chair, and she discussed them with Shimin. Shimin did not enjoy teaching anyway, so the chair and Shimin thought it would be best if he would not teach the following semester and instead became a teaching assistant for a professor. His duties would be grading exams and homework. This suited him much better, and Shimin was quite efficient at his task, earning the respect of his professor.

Shimin's academic performance was superior as well. He earned excellent grades in his graduate classes and he finished his master's thesis on time. In fact, everyone, including his advisor, was quite surprised he had completed his thesis and was asking for an appropriate date for his defense. He had met with his advisor a minimal number of times, although he did send his advisor a memo once a month about his progress on his thesis. Most other students work closely with their thesis advisors and meet with them frequently. In recommendation letters that were sent out to prospective employers, Shimin's advisor noted how independent he was.

Not surprisingly, Shimin was a superior student before graduate school, in both high school and college. In high school, he was an "ideal" student. He completed his assignments diligently, aced his exams, and was never disruptive in class. In fact, he rarely spoke in class unless he was asked a direct question and then usually answered correctly. He gained a reputation for being self-motivated. His teachers and guidance counselors did not need to spend much time with him because he always worked things out on his own. He actually preferred things that way because he felt he could always depend on himself but that one could not always depend on someone else's help. One reason he could rely so much on himself to learn and to make decisions was because he was an avid reader and computer whiz. He could do research in the library or on the Internet on something and not need to discuss it with anyone else or ask anyone questions.

This same pattern of behavior continued in college with Shimin excelling academically, despite being an international student from Hong Kong in the United States whose second language was English. One professor who did begin to get to know Shimin suggested that he needed to contribute more to class discussion. This was a disturbing concept to Shimin, who until then had used his academic success to discourage interaction with others. He thought that if one doesn't have any questions, one didn't need to talk in class. Shimin dismissed this idea of talking in class as being an idiosyncrasy of the professor. Certainly, independence and self-sufficiency was much better and would earn him other's respect, he believed.

Shimin has not had much of a social life by his own choosing. He rarely dates. Although he says (and believes) that this is because he is too busy, it is actually because he hates the process of getting to know someone. He is reluctant to talk about himself and finds it difficult to avoid answering questions about himself on first dates. He did not get to know many other students in college or graduate school because he did not live in the dorms. He preferred to rent an apartment so that he could live on his own. In both college and graduate school, Shimin joined various clubs and organizations, but again, he rarely made it to the meetings because he was "too busy."

Application Questions

Using Horney's psychoanalytic social theory, analyze Shimin's behavior by answering the following questions.

    1. How does Shimin combat basic anxiety according to Horney's theory?

    2. Which of Horney's neurotic needs does Shimin display?

    3. Which of Horney's secondary defenses is Shimin using when he says he is too busy to join clubs or go on dates? Why?

Theory Comparison Questions

1. Use another theory, besides Horney's, to explain Shimin's antisocial behavior.

2. How do Horney's and Fromm's emphasis on social influences on behavior compare?

3. How does Adler's concept of social interest compare with Horney's concept of withdrawing from others? Use both of these concepts to explain Shimin's avoidance of close relationships.

Fromm

Case Study 11

It is Christmas Eve and Jeff is basking in the glow of the Christmas tree and fire in the fireplace. As he looks around the living room of his parents' house, he can actually see the love of his family, and he smiles to himself. His parents are on the floor playing with their grandchildren, his children, and as he and his wife enter the living room with Christmas cookies and cocoa, the children rush for the snack squealing with excitement. It is like this every winter holiday season. Jeff and his wife, Ann, travel six hours by car with their children to spend a week with Jeff's parents. This is a daunting task. Jeff and Ann have to pack clothes not only for themselves but also for their children. When the children were younger, this also meant packing bottles, nipples, diapers, bibs, and so forth, which were the every-day needs of babies and toddlers, along with snacks, toys, and books to help keep the children amused during the long ride to Grandma and Grandpa's. Finally, there were all the Christmas presents. This seemed to be the hardest task, especially when the children were younger and they all believed in Santa Claus. It was diffi-cult to hide the presents in such a packed and cramped car and to shuffle the pres-ents inside his parent's house before Christmas to set them up for Christmas morning. There was also the occasional lake-effect snow that sometimes hit at this time of year and that could make driving treacherous. Still, neither he nor his wife would miss this event for anything. During the holiday season, they would be able to visit with many relatives they can see only this one time each year. On Christmas Day and New Year's Day, his parents, Jeff's family, and his brother's and sister's families would get together, feast, and talk. And, all the children—the cousins—would get to know each other again and play together with their new toys.

Returning to his hometown was meaningful to Jeff and to his wife. For Jeff returning to his hometown helped him reconnect to the person he was when he was growing up. Although Ann was not from Jeff's hometown of Batavia, she had no real family and was accepted readily into Jeff's family when they became engaged years ago. Returning to Batavia each winter was enjoyable for Ann, and to Jeff, because they saw so little of their family and because they had no family that lived near them. Jeff and Ann had some close friends but no blood relatives living nearby. Sometimes they felt lonely, especially when they heard of their friends being assisted by their families who were located nearby. This was especially true when their children were very small and babysitters did not show up when they were supposed to. Ann and Jeff often had to scramble for a sitter so they could both go to work. They also would have liked to spend a little more time alone as a couple and wished some family members were around to watch the kids and give them this opportunity. Beyond having trustworthy babysitters, Jeff and Ann wished they could share some of the everyday events of life with family. They wished Jeff's parents could see their grandchildren in school plays and little league. For Ann and Jeff, family has always been important, and they wanted to instill this value in their children. Jeff remembers the holiday seasons when he was growing up and how his family always had Thanksgiving dinner with his cousins' family and how Christmas and New Year's were also shared with others. He wanted his children to have these kind of enjoyable memories when they grew up. Likewise, Jeff and Ann wanted their children to understand where they came from and be aware of their cultural heritage.

The loneliness of living away from family made Jeff and Ann sometimes consider moving back to the small town outside of Rochester where Jeff grew up, especially when they first moved to Cleveland. This was not a realistic consideration, however; it was more of a wish. There were no job opportunities in Batavia in Jeff's type of work, and Ann was settled in her career as well. Although exciting, the move to Cleveland had also been frightening for both Ann and Jeff. They initially thought that the move would be good for them, and their new marriage, because there would be no family influences, but it was also stressful and scary to be completely on their own. They had no one to ask advice from about houses they considered buying or other such decisions.

Jeff and Ann did well on their own, with minimal hassles, however, and both found their work rewarding and were optimistic about continuing their work. Jeff worked for Alcoa, an aluminum company that is also known for recycling, and felt good about his efforts that sometimes resulted in a better environment. The company encouraged its workers to come up with ideas that would benefit the company and the environment. His latest project was developing a new method to manufacture aluminum wheels. Ann was a computer programmer and enjoyed the daily challenges of creating new programs that made other people's work easier. They were both aware that they had unique talents that benefited their employers and felt confident in their positions, despite the popular trend of downsizing.

Likewise, Jeff and Ann's marriage was strong. No family is perfect and theirs was no exception; there were the usual squabbles among children and arguments revolving around money and housekeeping. Nevertheless, Jeff and Ann truly cared about each other and about their children, and their children similarly loved their parents and their siblings. Jeff and Ann had similar views about how to live their lives to make them meaningful and tried to instill their value system into their children. In particular, Jeff and Ann wanted their children to believe that it was important to somehow make the world a better place than the way they found it. Both

Jeff and Ann believed that their work did this, and they hoped that their children would eventually find work that was meaningful as well.

Application Questions

Using Fromm's humanistic psychoanalytic theory, analyze Jeff and Ann's behavior by answering the following questions.

1. How could Fromm's theory explain Jeff and Ann's return to Batavia every holiday season despite the hardships?

2. Why do people in general and Jeff and Ann, in particular, marry or form other close relationships, according to Fromm's theory?

3. What is the transcendence need according to Fromm? Has it been fulfilled by Ann and Jeff? Why?

4. What is the identity need according to Fromm? Has it been fulfilled by Ann and Jeff? Why?

5. What is the excitation and stimulation need according to Fromm? Has it been fulfilled by Ann and Jeff? Why?

6. What is Jeff and Ann's frame of orientation, according to Fromm's theory?

7. What character orientation, according to Fromm, would Ann and Jeff belong to?

8. How could Fromm's theory explain Jeff and Ann's mixed feelings about initially moving to Cleveland?

Theory Comparison Questions

1. How do Fromm's needs compare with Rogers's needs? With Maslow's?

2. How could behaviorism explain Jeff and Ann's return to Batavia every holiday season? How does the motivation for behavior emphasized by behaviorism compare with that of Fromm's theory?

3. How could sociobiology explain Ann and Jeff getting married and having children? How does this explanation compare with that of Fromm?

Fromm

Case Study 12

Andrea is about to embark on an obligatory visit to her remaining family for a week. She visits once a year, and every year she dreads it. Each visit is stressful, and once she arrives at her mother's house she feels like an outsider. It seems as though Andrea was always the outsider, even as a child. Her sister Marla was the favored daughter and seemed to encourage the favoritism by doing whatever their mother wanted instead of fulfilling her own needs and developing her own personality. Andrea, on the other hand, often irritated her mother because she insisted on doing things her way as a child. Even as an adult, Andrea continued to behave in certain ways their mother disapproved of. It wasn't that Andrea wanted to have harmful or damaging experiences; she just wanted to do all the things that other children, and later, young adults, always wanted to do. She wanted to go out with friends, have a few drinks, dance, and so on, but her mother disapproved of this behavior. It wasn't that her mother said anything. It was more an unspoken message conveyed by a disapproving look or tone of voice. Marla, on the other hand, did not want to risk this subtle form of disapproval and so rarely went out. Over time, Andrea's mother seemed to have gained more control over Marla's behavior and their relationship had deepened into an unhealthy dependence.

Today, when Andrea visits she feels left out, as though Marla and her mother have formed a clique that Andrea is not part of. When Marla and her mother talk, they look directly at each other, as though they are only talking to each other, even though Andrea is in the room. They even consult each other about whether they should have a snack and sometimes share cups of coffee. Although Marla has her own home, she and her mother see each other everyday after work and have dinner together, sometimes at the mother's house, sometimes at Marla's house. They have keys to each other's houses and let themselves in whenever it suits them. All these activities ostracize Andrea and make her feel uncomfortable.

It pains Andrea to see how dependent Marla is on their mother, and she wishes her sister had a different kind of life. Yet, nothing Andrea does seems to lessen the bond between Marla and her mother. When Andrea still lived at home, she would ask Marla to go out with her and her friends, but most times Marla refused to go. When Andrea moved away from her hometown, she would invite Marla down for a visit, but inevitably Marla assumed that their mother was invited too and they would visit together. This inability to travel without her mother began years ago. When Andrea graduated from college, she wanted to treat herself to a vacation and had arranged for her and Marla to go to Maine. Then, as they were discussing the vacation over coffee at their mother's house, their mother had mentioned that she wished she could go. Marla, without consulting Andrea, asked their mother to join them. Their mother immediately jumped at the chance, and the three of them traveled together. This was very disappointing for Andrea who was looking forward to going on her first vacation without a parent. From her perspective, the vacation was a disaster. After they went out the first night of vacation with some of the fellow travelers their age for drinks, Marla and Andrea walked into the room they shared with their mother to disapproving looks. Their mother was sitting in a chair, frowning, and expressed how worried she was about them. That was the last outing they had with the other young people. For the rest of the trip, Marla and their mother paired off and seemed to exclude Andrea; she felt like a third wheel, even though she was the one who initiated the vacation. Even today, at the age of 35, Marla still only goes on vacation with her mother. Likewise, she often invites her mother to go out with her and the few friends she sees occasionally. Andrea has given up trying to do things alone with Marla. Discussing the relationship between Marla and her mother is out of the question because Marla rebuffs any attempt at this type of conversation.

Other things also bother Andrea about her family visits. For example, she is often bored. Neither her mother nor her sister is very busy. Their main activities are working at their jobs and spending time with each other. Andrea, on the other hand enjoys going shopping and going to restaurants, museums, and other cultural activities. She frequently goes out on weekends, whereas her family rarely does. This lack of activity places a lot of pressure on Andrea. Because she only visits once a year, her mother and her sister assume that she will spend all her time with them. But, she would like to see a few friends that she grew up with on her visit as well. Unfortunately, just as when she was younger, she faces disapproval when she tries to see other people besides her sister and her mother. She wishes her family would be more active and her sister would be more independent.

Application Questions

Using Fromm's humanistic psychoanalytic theory, analyze Marla's behavior by answering the following questions.

1. What type of mother fixation could describe the relationship between Marla and her mother, according to Fromm? According to the theory, why is this behavior displayed?

2. What character orientation, according to Fromm's theory, would best describe Marla?

3. Which of Fromm's existential needs are met for Marla? Which are not? Explain.

4. Which mechanism of escape from freedom has Marla adopted? Why?

Theory Comparison Questions

1. What other theories, besides Fromm's, could explain Marla's relationship with her mother? How?

2. Compare Horney's concept of submissiveness to combat basic anxiety with Fromm's concept of submitting to another to fulfill the relatedness need. Apply both of these concepts to Marla's relationship with her mother.

3. How does an excessively dependent personality (or character) develop, according to Freudian theory? How could these concepts explain Marla's relationship with her mother? How do Fromm's character orientations compare with Freud's? How do these concepts compare with traits in trait theories?

Sullivan

Case Study 13

Stacy, Caucasian and 26 years old, is a waitress. She is very good at what she does, primarily because she is so preoccupied with making sure all her customer's needs are met, even when they seem to be unreasonable. Her boss likes that about her because she keeps the customers happy. An example that illustrates her skill involves a customer who had placed an order for country-fried steak. When she brought it to him, he was dissatisfied with just about everything about it: He asked for more gravy on both his meat and mashed potatoes; he demanded a larger portion of vegetables, extra rolls, and that the entire order be heated up more. Stacy apologized profusely and brought back an order that was much more to his liking. She didn't even bat an eye. Most of the other waitresses she worked with would have brought him his order back but would have found other ways to get back at this customer, for example by taking their time in getting him his check at the end of the meal, and certainly they would not have apologized to him because there really was nothing wrong with the order.

Stacy was used to trying to please others. She had been doing it her entire life. As a child, throughout adolescence, and now throughout young adulthood, Stacy had always been submissive, sometimes to the point that others found her annoying.

Being the third of four children raised by a single mother, Stacy craved her mom's attention but rarely received it. Her two older brothers were quite rambunctious and seemed to be always getting into some kind of trouble that their mother had to help get them out of. Her younger sister was born only 13 months after Stacy, six months after their father had left them. Although their mother loved them all, she found it difficult to give all her children the attention they needed and wanted. This was especially true of Stacy, who experienced the prototypical middle-child syndrome: Her older siblings were demanding of their mother's attention and used to getting it, and her younger sister needed their mother's attention because she was a baby. This did not leave much time for Stacy.

When Stacy did get her mother's attention as a preschool-aged child, it was often precisely because she was not demanding it. Her mother would often make comments to Stacy such as, "Thank goodness you aren't asking me to do something too!" Although this does not sound endearing, Stacy's mother always said it with a sense of humor, and it did not hurt Stacy's feelings but, rather, made her feel good. Like all children, Stacy also wanted to please her mother and would often do things like try to help her mom clean the kitchen or help with her baby sister. When Stacy did this, her mother would give her a rare hug and thank her. What Stacy learned from these experiences was that to gain someone else's attention or love, one needed to not make demands and, instead, do things for that person.

This submissive pattern of behavior continued into the realm of school and friendships. Stacy was an average student in early grade school. She was quiet in school and rarely volunteered in class or demanded the teacher's time. She also had some difficulty establishing friendships with the other children. She was hesitant in approaching them and asking them to play with her. As a method to fit in with the other children, she would always play whatever they wanted and how they wanted, regardless of whether she wanted to or not. Not surprisingly, the other kids tolerated Stacy but often took advantage of her, giving her the roles to play in their games that were most undesirable, such as the bad guys while the other children played the roles of good guys like cops or super heroes. Other children had best friends, but Stacy did not.

In later grade school, she also had trouble forming friendships with the other girls. It wasn't that they really disliked her. She just never initiated any contact with them. The other girls called each other and invited each other over to their houses, but Stacy never took these initiatives.

In junior high, Stacy became interested in boys, just like the other girls did. Like the other girls, she read magazines that included stories about girls having relationships with boys. These stories had a similar theme: In them, the girl often required a boy's help to solve a problem. When he solved the problem, he became interested in the girl. Or, by the girls changing in such a way that pleased the boys, the girls were able to establish relationships with them. Once again, Stacy learned that doing what others wanted is what gets them to like you and become your friend or boyfriend. Stacy became increasingly attractive during adolescence. This physical attractiveness, along with the boys thinking that Stacy was very agreeable, allowed Stacy to begin romantic relationships. Because of Stacy's inability to assert herself, she began to have sex shortly after beginning to date. When her boyfriends asked her for sex, she often agreed because she was afraid they would leave if she did not. Unfortunately, they often broke off the relationship anyway. Shortly after a break up, another boy would ask Stacy out. She was getting a reputation for being promiscuous.

These types of relationships continued in high school and, in one case, resulted in unfortunate consequences. Stacy met a young man while she was in high school, and initially she was pleased with their relationship. The one thing she did not like or understand was his temper. He would often lose his temper and blame Stacy for whatever it was that set him off. Initially, his outbursts only involved yelling but eventually escalated into pushing and shoving and finally other more serious forms of physical abuse. While Stacy was in this relationship, she continually tried to please her boyfriend and wondered what it was that she was doing wrong. Stacy's mother put a stop to the relationship by forbidding them to see each other after she had seen the bruises on Stacy's body.

Now as an adult, Stacy is still searching for an intimate relationship. She still does not have any female friends, partly because she does not initiate friendships and partly because the other women she works with do not initiate them, either. Although they don't mind working with Stacy, they view her as a kind of wimp. Likewise, although she dates, her relationships with men do not last long because they feel as though they cannot get to know Stacy if she is continually trying to do only things that they like to do and talk about things that they want to talk about. They feel as though the relationship is very one-sided and this makes them uncomfortable.

Application Questions

Using Sullivan's interpersonal personality theory, analyze Stacy's behavior by answering the following questions.

1. How could Stacy's interactions be characterized? How could these interactions be considered "personality" according to Sullivan's theory?

2. What did Stacy experience during Sullivan's juvenile era? How did these experiences affect her personality?

3. What did Stacy experience during Sullivan's Preadolescence Stage? How did these experiences affect her personality?

4. What did Stacy experience during Sullivan's Early Adolescence Stage? How did these experiences affect her personality?

5. What did Stacy experience during Sullivan's Late Adolescence Stage? How did these experiences affect her personality?

6. What did Stacy experience during Sullivan's Adulthood Stage? How did these experiences affect her personality?

7. What would Stacy have to do to form a true relationship, according to Sullivan's theory?

8. Which of Sullivan's needs were fulfilled for Stacy?

Theory Comparison Questions

1. Which other theories, besides Sullivan's, could also explain Stacy's behavior? How?

2. How could evolutionary psychology explain Stacy's relationships with males? How does this compare with Sullivan's explanation?

3. According to Maslow, which of Stacy's needs have been fulfilled? How do Maslow's needs compare with Sullivan's?

Sullivan

Case Study 14

As Brian approaches his sixth birthday, his mother Tammy reflects on the changes in Brian over the last six years.

Brian was a demanding baby. As a first-time mother, Tammy wanted to do everything right and so had tried to nurse Brian. Unfortunately, Tammy was not prepared for how long it took to breast-feed and the discomfort that is initially involved. It seemed like she started out with cracked nipples. While still in the hospital, Brian often latched onto Tammy's breast incorrectly, which resulted in her having bruised and cracked nipples that took time to heal. Sometimes Brian would refuse to nurse because he preferred the ease of sucking from a bottle, which nurses introduced him to in the hospital nursery. Even though Tammy eventually began to learn how to position Brian and how to get him to latch on correctly, nursing just wasn't comfortable for her. She hated having leaking breasts; even nursing pads didn't always help. She was exhausted from a difficult delivery and from the physical demands of producing enough milk to keep Brian satisfied. And he seemed to need a lot of milk. Brian nursed every couple of hours for 40 minutes each time, even at night. Because Tammy was the sole nighttime feeder, she only got an hour of sleep at a time. In fact, the first night home from the hospital, Brian was up just about all night. That, coupled with being in labor for 19 hours and the hospital staff waking Tammy every couple of hours to take her temperature and blood pressure, made Tammy feel brain-dead a couple of days after Brian was born. She began to feel resentful toward her husband who was getting more sleep than she and who was not in such physical pain, and she began to wonder whether nursing was worth the effort. The lack of sleep and the discomfort of nursing combined to form a fairly unpleasant experience as she fed her child. After just two months, Tammy gave up nursing and bottle-fed Brian, who had no trouble adjusting to bottles. When she started bottle-feeding, Tammy was amazed at how much better she felt, how much more energy she had, and how enjoyable feeding Brian was. She was able to relax when she fed him and gazed at his round little face, often smiling to herself and to Brian.

Brian was a difficult baby in other ways as well. He did not sleep through the night regularly until he was past two years old. Much of his waking was probably caused by teething pain. Tammy and her husband, Phil, often joked about Brian's "witching hour": the time every evening when Brian would begin to cry uncontrollably and nothing they would do could calm him down. And, he could scream loud. They tried holding him, singing to him, walking him; nothing worked. He did not stop crying until he fell asleep for the night. Looking back on that experience, Tammy wonders if Brian had actually been hungry but, at the time, neither parent thought that was possible because he had eaten so recently before the onset of the crying fit.

As he grew older, Brian became increasingly cooperative. When he was three and a half or four, and talking adequately, Tammy was able to talk to Brian about his temper tantrums and various other unacceptable behaviors. Sometimes Brian would refer to himself as the bad Brian or the good Brian. On the days he was in an agreeable mood he would tell his mother that the "good Brian was here today." Now that he is approaching the age of six, however, he no longer refers to himself as two people.

Brian is turning out to be quite different than what he was as a baby. He is a confident, personable, intelligent little boy with a wonderful sense of humor. He also has quite an imagination. The latest item he has conjured up is "ghost monsters" who drink juice when no one is looking. When Tammy asks him "who did something" in the house, Brian's standard reply is "a ghost monster." This started when Brian was about four. He would forget that he drank all his juice, and when he went back for more, he would wonder where it had gone. He started blaming ghost monsters. Eventually, the ghost monsters took on their own characteristics. One had black, bushy hair and red eyes. Some were friendly; others were not. Not too long ago, Tammy heard Brian talking to his little sister about how they should have a tea party with the friendly ghost monsters.

The last six years have certainly been eventful, but Tammy would not change any of it.

Application Questions

Using Sullivan's interpersonal personality theory, analyze Tammy's and Brian's behavior by answering the following questions.

1. What is a personification according to Sullivan? Find examples of the good mother, bad mother, good me, and bad me in the case study.

2. Using Sullivan's theory, interpret Tammy and Brian's feeding experiences.

3. How could Sullivan's theory interpret Brian's "witching hour" and his subsequent falling asleep?

4. In which of Sullivan's stages would you place Brian? Why?

5. What level of cognition does Brian display according to Sullivan's theory? Why? When did he begin to display this level?

Theory Comparison Questions

1. How does Klein's discussion of the mother's breast as both good and bad compare with Sullivan's good mother/bad mother personification?

2. Use Bandura's concept of reciprocal determinism to explain Tammy and Brian's breastfeeding experiences. How does this compare with Sullivan's explanation?

3. Use Skinner's radical behaviorism to explain Tammy and Brian's breastfeeding experiences. How does this compare with Sullivan's explanation?

Maslow

Case Study 15

Cindy is a four-year-old who has had a troubling childhood. She was taken away from her parents and placed in a foster home when she was only six months old. Her pediatrician contacted Children and Youth Services because she was concerned that Cindy was being neglected. When the pediatrician first saw Cindy (and on subsequent occasions), Cindy appeared unkempt and had an odor that suggested that she had not been washed recently. Likewise, the physician was also concerned about neglect because of Cindy's lack of growth. At the first checkup, which usually occurs when the baby is about two weeks old, Cindy had not gained a sufficient amount of weight. Babies usually lose a few ounces during their stay in the hospital, but they are expected to regain that weight (and sometimes more) by the time they are two weeks old. Cindy was four weeks old at her first checkup and had gained back the weight she had lost in the hospital but not any additional weight. Cindy had also not gained adequate weight at her six-week checkup (which actually occurred at nine weeks). It did not appear that physical reasons were the cause of the lack of growth. Rather, when the pediatrician asked how much formula the baby was given, it was not an adequate amount. The physician reprimanded the adult with Cindy (her grandmother) and instructed her on the amount of formula necessary for a child that age. However, at her three-month checkup, which was also late, Cindy still was not growing adequately. At this third visit, Cindy also had a terrible diaper rash. Her skin was so raw that in some places it was raised up, indicating a yeast infection. The severity of the diaper rash alarmed the pediatrician. Usually parents brought their babies in before a diaper rash became that bad, but the physician hadn't even met the parents. Instead, Cindy's maternal grandmother had brought her in on each occasion. The woman was quite elderly with severe arthritis, but she made the effort to bring Cindy in because of the diaper rash. Although the grandmother was not Cindy's caregiver, she thought it was important for the child to receive the usual immunization shots and to be checked periodically by a physician—that is, whenever the grandmother was physically able to make the visits. Cindy's caregiver was actually her mother. When the pediatrician asked why the mother did not accompany Cindy to these

visits, the grandmother just said that she was not available. The physician therefore suspected that Cindy was being neglected by her mother. She did not seem to
be receiving adequate nutrition or hygiene.

When Children and Youth Services personnel investigated, they found that
Cindy was born to a 40-year-old mother who was a drug addict and who had no
interest in rehabilitation. She was a single mother who did not have a home of her
own but instead lived with friends. These friends lived in a relatively poor neighborhood that housed primarily African Americans and Latinos. Cindy and her
mother were also African American. They would live at one friend's place for a
while and then move on to another friend who would put them up for a while.
Occasionally, they would visit and live with Cindy's grandmother. On these occasions, the grandmother brought Cindy to the pediatrician but Cindy's grandmother
was elderly and sickly and so could not take care of the strenuous physical needs
of an infant. No one knew who Cindy's father was, and there were no other relatives.

Although Children and Youth Services attempted to intervene on Cindy's
behalf with her mother by providing education and parent training, her mother's
drug addiction prevented adequate care. On one occasion, when the caseworker
visited Cindy and her mother, Cindy was so severely dehydrated that she was in
medical danger. When asked about the cause, Cindy's mother replied that it was
"just the flu" and that medical attention was not needed. When pressed, Cindy's
mother refused to take her to a doctor or hospital, stating that she did not have the
money to do so. In actuality, Cindy's mother was in need of a fix and preferred to
use the money for that. So, Cindy was placed in a foster home.

Although there are many loving foster homes, Cindy unfortunately was placed
in one where she received adequate nutrition, physical care, and shelter but little
else. Her foster family was more concerned about receiving adequate compensation for their foster care than they were with the welfare of the child. Her foster
parents showed her little affection, rarely holding her or talking to her. Over the
course of a few months, the neighborhood in which she and her foster family lived
deteriorated, and gang violence, including drive-by shootings, began. The foster
family decided to move to another state and did not want to adopt Cindy. Her
caseworker was notified, and Cindy was to be placed with another foster family.
Contact with Cindy's biological mother was sporadic, and Cindy could not be
placed back with her mother because of the mother's continued drug addiction.

At the age of 12 months, Cindy looked as though she was only 6 months old
and although she could sit up on her own, she still hadn't started to crawl, let alone
walk. She cringed at someone's touch, having gotten very little during her first
year of life. She also seemed very shy and uncertain of herself. She became frightened and cried easily. Although Cindy's material needs were met, her lack of interaction with people and lack of love from her foster and biological families did not
allow her to thrive.

The caseworker placed Cindy with another foster family. Fortunately for
Cindy, this family was very caring. They lived in a clean, quiet, working-class
neighborhood where other small children lived and were being raised. Her new

foster mother stayed home with Cindy and her two biological daughters, aged 5 and 8, during the day; she also worked part time at a catalog company taking orders over the phone four evenings a week after her husband came home. Cindy's new foster father worked as a supervisor at a warehouse that distributed nonfood items to supermarkets. Both foster parents were very patient and showed affection readily. Their two daughters were thrilled to have a baby sister to help take care of. Although Cindy was very tentative at first, she gradually began to seek out physical contact, especially when she was frightened or not feeling well. Within eight weeks, Cindy had grown and developed enough to look like a 9-month-old. Within six months, Cindy had caught up developmentally and physically with other children her age. During this time, Cindy's mother overdosed and died. Because no other family members were willing or able to take care of Cindy, she was put up for adoption. Fortunately for Cindy, her foster family members had grown to love her so much that they applied to adopt her and were granted their request. Cindy now lives with her adopted family and is a happy, confident, 4-year-old little girl.

Application Questions

Using Maslow's holistic-dynamic theory, analyze Cindy's life by answering the following questions.

1. Consider Maslow's hierarchy of needs during Cindy's first year of life. Which needs were fulfilled? Which were not?

2. What was the outcome of the needs being fulfilled or not fulfilled?

3. Which of Maslow's needs were fulfilled for Cindy during her second year of life? What was the outcome of that?

4. What type of values would Cindy have to embrace to actualize?

Theory Comparison Questions

1. How do Maslow's safety needs compare with Erikson's concepts of learning basic trust in the oral sensory stage? Apply this concept for Cindy's experience, explaining what crisis can lead to basic trust and whether it was developed for Cindy.

2. How do Sullivan's concepts of needs differ from Maslow's? Which of Sullivan's needs were met for Cindy before and after her adoption? Which were not?

3. How does Horney's concept of basic anxiety compare with Maslow's safety needs and love needs? Apply this concept to Cindy's experiences before and after her adoption.

Maslow

Case Study 16

Frank is a 42-year-old, Native American, factory worker, who is married and has two kids. He lives in a small town in western Pennsylvania that is located about an hour away from the nearest major city. The factory he works at manufactures chairs. He has been working the graveyard shift (11 P.M. to 7 A.M.) for about six years now. The hours are terrible, and he has never really gotten used to them. He tries to sleep when he gets home in the early morning but finds it difficult because his kids are getting ready for school at that time and his wife is getting ready for work. Even if he waits to go to bed until everyone leaves the house, Frank still has trouble sleeping in the daylight. He is tired all the time, but at least he gets some sleep on weekends and the money earned working the third shift is better than that of the first or second shift. Sometimes he thinks that if he could just get enough sleep, he would be a truly happy man.

Frank and his wife have been able to support their family between their two incomes. They have been able to buy a small house; there is always food on the table; and their kids have decent clothes to wear. The house, the clothes, and the food are not fancy but always adequate. That is, Frank and his wife have been able to support their family until recently. Frank has just lost his job. Frank's plant had been bought out by a rival out-of-state company and initially, there seemed to be no change in the production schedule. Then one Friday, Frank received a notice in his paycheck telling him that this was his last day of work and asking him to take all his personal effects with him. The factory was to be closed immediately because of the buy-out. Frank was devastated by the news, as were his co-workers. The workers were also surprised by the news. It seemed as though the chair company had always been there, and they thought it always would be. Their fathers had worked at, and retired from, the company. Some of the workers' grandfathers did too. They thought that their jobs were secure. They were wrong.

Frank and his co-workers had always taken pride in their work. They crafted their chairs by hand, using tools their fathers had used before them. They produced an excellent product. Frank was especially proud of the intricate designs he made on the back of the chairs he produced. His skill earned him the respect of his co-workers. Now, two months after the closing, Frank is not proud of very much. He has not been able to find any other work, and he is embarrassed by the prospect of not being able to support his family. Although he and his wife have been able to make ends meet temporarily because of her job and his unemployment compensation, he is not sure what will happen when his unemployment compensation runs out. How will they pay their mortgage? How will they put food on the table? How could they possibly save for their children's college education?

Depending on his wife's income has been especially hard on Frank. He believes that he should be the breadwinner, but his wife has been incredibly supportive since the plant closing. She is constantly trying to boost his self-esteem and has never complained once about the things they have had to give up. He loves her terribly and wishes he could do more for her and for his children whom he adores. He would give anything to go back to being tired all the time, if he could have his job back. He feels useless and incompetent.

Application Questions

Using Maslow's holistic-dynamic theory, analyze Frank's life by answering the following questions.

1. Which of Maslow's needs, described in his hierarchy, were met for Frank before he was laid off? Give examples of how they were met.

2. Which needs were not met before Frank was laid off? Why?

3. Which of Maslow's needs were met for Frank after he was laid off? Give examples of how they were met.

4. Which needs were not met after Frank was laid off? Why?

Theory Comparison Questions

1. How do Maslow's needs compare with those discussed by Rogers? Which of Rogers's needs were met for Frank before he was laid off? After he was laid off?

2. How do the Maslow's needs compare with those discussed by Fromm? Which of Fromm's needs were met for Frank before he was laid off? After he was laid off?

3. How could Kelly's modulation corollary and concept of permeability explain Frank's feelings of uselessness and incompetence after the loss of his job? How does the focus of Kelly's theory differ from that of Maslow's?

Rogers
Case Study 17

Katharine is scheduled to attend her 20th high school reunion next month and is looking forward to it. She had missed her 10th high school reunion purposefully because she had felt like such a failure. She was afraid that her old classmates would have accomplished much more than she had. Even worse, she was afraid that they would feel sorry for her.

Just before her 10th reunion, Katharine had been divorced, and she was working as a secretary to support herself. Katharine had married her high school sweetheart the year after they graduated. She had always wanted to be married; as a child, she dreamt of it. So, when her boyfriend asked her to get married, she happily agreed. But, marriage was not everything she had dreamed it would be. In high school she had dreams of also owning her own business, but her husband disapproved of her taking business courses at the local community college and discouraged any attempts she made at earning money on her own. He wanted a wife who stayed home and took care of him and his house. The marriage was also disappointing because even though they tried, she had been unable to become pregnant. The marriage ended when her husband began an affair with a co-worker and asked her for a divorce so that he could marry his new love. Katharine was devastated. She had no husband, no children, and no career. She had never imagined herself in that position. In high school, she had always thought she would be one of those women who had it all: a career and family life. Now she was a secretary in someone else's business with no family possibilities in sight. To make matters worse, Katharine had gained 30 pounds the year after she was divorced. Katharine had always been slender, and she had no intentions of going to her reunion looking like that.

A co-worker noted Katharine's depression after her divorce and suggested that she accompany her to her Women's Support Group. The support group changed Katharine's life. The other women in the group listened to what she said and seemed to understand what she was going through. As she continued to go to the group, and as she learned that they would not pity her or make fun of her, she opened up more and discussed her feelings. Eventually she told them about her high school dream of owning her own business. She had been reluctant to discuss this with them at first because her ex-husband had always made fun of her when she brought up the possibility. Instead of criticism, she received support from her group.

They encouraged her to take a few business courses and discussed with her what type of business she could open. When they found out that she was artistic, they suggested that she try making and selling some crafts at various craft shows. Katharine did just that, experimenting with various floral arrangements, Christmas decorations, and knick-knacks on weekends and evenings. Although these items sold, she did not sell enough of them to be able to support herself and start her own business. She didn't find her niche until she started woodworking. She began making Victorian-looking Santas out of wood and hand painting them. They had Katharine's own unique touches. She was surprised to sell out her inventory on the second day of a three-day craft show. This gave her the confidence she needed. Katharine built up her inventory and rented a small storefront where she began to sell her Santas. Eventually, she was making enough to be able to quit her secretary job and devote her whole attention to her business. Her items became so popular that she had to employ two other people to keep up with her orders.

Opening her business had other positive effects as well. Her business had kept her so busy that she did not always have time to eat, so Katharine lost 20 of the 30 pounds she had gained after her divorce. Socially, she saw more people such as her "regulars," customers who came back repeatedly. In fact, one customer she met at her shop asked her out, and their relationship had blossomed to the extent that they were married. She also felt needed because she had two co-workers who depended on her. She depended on them as well, and they occasionally came up with good suggestions for their store. She even became active in the local chamber of commerce. Katharine no longer feels like a failure and is confident about attending her 20th reunion.

Application Questions

Using Rogers's person-centered theory, explain Katherine's behavior by answering the following questions.

1. How did Katharine's self-concept differ from her ideal self before her experience with her support group? What does this imply about her mental health, according to Rogers's theory?

2. How could Rogerian theory explain any difference in Katharine's selves?

3. How did Katharine's self-concept differ from her ideal self after her experience with her support group? What does this imply about her mental health, according to Rogers's theory?

4. According to Rogerian theory, what made the difference in congruence before and after Katharine's experience with her support group?

Theory Comparison Questions

1. What other theories, besides Rogers's, could be applied to Katherine's experiences to explain them? How?

2. Apply Bandura's concepts of self-regulation and self-efficacy to Katherine's experiences. How does the focus of Bandura's theory differ from that of Rogers's?

3. How do the needs discussed by Rogers compare with those discussed by Fromm? By Maslow?

Rogers
Case Study 18

Allen works assembling cars at the Saturn plant in Spring Hill, Tennessee. His job is a good one: He earns a decent salary; has help from the company for purchasing such benefits as health insurance and retirement; and his supervisor treats him and his co-workers well, asking their opinions about how to make their work run smoother and more efficiently. As he approaches the age of 30, however, he has become increasingly dissatisfied with his work life. He wishes that he could do something more fulfilling and more meaningful.

When he was younger, Allen dreamed of becoming a teacher. He was a pretty good student in grade school and high school, and he had always loved children. Even as a child himself, Allen loved to play with the younger kids on his street, and they loved to play with him. During the summer, the younger kids would come down to his house and Allen would construct elaborate scenarios for the children to act out. They would play pirates, or cops and robbers, or have pretend jousting matches as medieval knights had done. In high school, Allen had decided to attend college and become a grade school teacher.

Allen's family was a typical working class family in the 1970s and 1980s. They had not been rich, but they had a decent home and enough food on the table and clothes on their backs. Although his parents did not really understand why Allen wanted to go to college, and they preferred that he would just find a decent job and settle down, they loved him and agreed to help Allen pay for tuition at the local college to help him fulfill his dream of becoming a teacher. So, Allen applied to the college and was accepted. He began attending and completed one semester but in the middle of that semester, his younger brother became very ill and required extensive medical treatment. Although Allen's father had some health insurance, it was not an adequate amount to cover the considerable medical bills. His parents told Allen that they would not be able to pay for his tuition anymore and pressured him into finding a job and contributing to the family financially. Under a great deal of stress, both Allen's father and mother expressed the notions that they thought that college was a waste of time and money, an excuse to not settle down and work. Luckily for Allen, the Saturn plant was just opening in his area. He applied for a position and was hired. A dutiful son, Allen, who was living at home, contributed part of his paycheck to his family to pay for his brother's medical expenses. His parents had always emphasized the importance of taking care of family when he was growing up and that was what Allen was trying to do.

A few months after beginning his job at the assembly plant, Allen's girlfriend, whom he had started dating in high school, became pregnant. Although they were careful, contraception does not work 100% effectively, and Allen and his girlfriend, Sue, had to make a decision about the pregnancy. Neither wanted to abort the child. Because they loved each other and had been seeing each other for almost three years, they decided to get married. Furthermore, Allen knew his parents would be very disapproving, perhaps even disown him, if he did not support and care for his child, and he was willing to do so. Their parents helped them with the expense of the wedding and setting up their own household. Although their parents would have preferred that the pregnancy come after the marriage, both sets of parents were thrilled with the prospect of becoming grandparents.

Allen and Sue set up house in a small apartment. It was comfortable, though sparsely furnished. Between Allen's salary and Sue's income as a part-time cashier at one of the local supermarkets, they were able to make ends meet and save a little money toward a down payment for a house. Sue quit her job to stay home with the baby, and Allen worked the occasional overtime to continue to earn enough to pay bills and save for a house. Eventually, they were able to buy a house and soon had another baby.

Allen was thrilled to be a father because he always had loved children. He was an affectionate father, loving spouse, and good provider. Supporting and caring for his family was important to him. But now, having been married for about 10 years, having his children in school, and approaching his 30th birthday, Allen feels some discontentment and anxiety. He wonders if there is anything else in life. He feels that if he is going to accomplish anything else, he needs to begin to work toward it now. And, he wonders if he should go back to school to earn his degree and get a job as a teacher. Sue was about to go back to work. With the kids in school now, she could work full time, have the grandparents watch the kids after school, and the money she would earn could be used to send Allen to college. But whenever Allen brings up the possibility of using the money to go back to school, Sue replies that the money could be used for better things than sending him to college, things like a new roof, new windows, a paved driveway, and better furniture. She does not understand why he would want to give up his job at the plant with its salary and benefits to find a job as a teacher. He is good at what he does. Allen's parents reiterate the same sentiments.

Besides talking to his wife and parents about his idea of becoming a teacher, Allen has tried to talk to some of his co-workers about it. They don't understand either. They think he would be crazy to give up his job. Good jobs are hard to come by. This isn't the first time Allen wasn't understood by his co-workers. Allen, who has always loved to read, would often read books or magazine articles and sometimes try to discuss them at work. His co-workers' responses were not very favorable, and sometimes they would laugh at some of the ideas he would bring up.

Although they liked Allen, they thought he was a little weird sometimes. Allen sometimes wondered if he was weird too. He didn't seem to fit in at work, and his wife and parents did not understand him. He sometimes felt that he wasn't who everybody thought he was. He thought he was a good worker, a good father, and a good husband, and that was how everyone else saw him as well. Allen, however, also saw himself as a college student, teacher, and mentor to children. He wished he could become that. He was proud of who he was now but that was not who he wanted to be.

Lately, Allen had been talking to one co-worker over lunch and breaks. Although most of his co-workers laughed at his ideas or told him they did not understand him, this one listened and supported him. Allen could say anything to this co-worker and not be afraid of being laughed at or criticized. This co-worker, who had had similar thoughts to Allen's years ago, seemed to know exactly what he was going through and helped Allen to see things more clearly. Sometimes the co-worker would repeat what Allen just said in a slightly different way, and Allen would suddenly have an insight. He felt as though he was growing as a person. Allen looked forward to these talks. They strengthened his resolve about becoming a teacher. He hopes that his parents and wife will accept him as he wants to be.

Application Questions

Using Rogers's person-centered theory, explain Allen's behavior by answering the following questions.

1. Which of Rogers's needs are fulfilled for Allen? Which are not met? Explain.
2. How does Allen's ideal self differ from his perceived self?
3. Why would Allen's organismic self be different than his perceived self?
4. The co-worker with whom Allen talks at lunch and breaks shares the characteristics of a Rogerian therapist. List them and explain how the co-worker displays them.
5. What would Allen have to do to actualize?

Theory Comparison Questions

1. How could Bandura's reciprocal determinism apply to Allen's experiences? How does the environmental factor in reciprocal determinism compare with Rogers's unconditional positive regard?

2. How could Skinner's radical behaviorism explain Allen's ambition to change careers? How does the focus of Skinner's theory compare with that of Rogers's?

3. How does Erikson's concept of identity, formed during the adolescent stage, apply to Allen's ambition to change careers? How does it compare with Rogers's self-concept?

Kelly

Case Study 19

Maria and Carlos have recently been blessed with their third child. They are in their late 20s and of Latino descent. After an uneventful pregnancy, Maria gave birth through a scheduled C-section to an 8 lb., 4 oz., healthy, baby girl. The C-section was scheduled after Maria had had two unscheduled C-sections with her other children. In both cases, Maria had gone through labor, dilated fully, and pushed for an extended period, but unfortunately, both babies were "stuck," and emergency C-sections were conducted. Maria thought long and hard about whether she should try to give birth vaginally this time or whether she should just schedule the C-section. In making this decision, Maria did a lot of research and reading. There were pros and cons on both sides. On the positive side: She would not have to go through labor, and she would know exactly when the baby was coming instead of waiting expectantly. On the negative side: She also knew that many C-sections are not necessary, that because it is major surgery there are increased risks, and that recovery from a C-section is usually tougher than from a vaginal birth. Finally, in consultation with her doctor, she decided to schedule the Caesarean. The whole procedure went well and now, as she thinks back reassessing her decision, she feels it was a good one.

Being a parent and spouse are two very important sources of identity for both Carlos and Maria. Maria and Carlos agreed about having a family even before they got married; in their pre-engagement discussions, they found that for both of them, being married and having children was a priority in life. Further, in these discussions, Maria and Carlos found out that their ideas about how to parent were quite similar, although there were also some differences. For example, both thought that being a parent would be fun and that playing with their children was just as important as caring for their physical needs, but Carlos thought that Maria should give up her job and stay home with the kids full time. Maria thought working part-time and putting the kids in day care about 20 hours a week would be good. They also differed on more minor issues such as whether the children should open Christmas presents on Christmas Eve or Christmas Day and whether grandparents should do any extensive amounts of babysitting. Both also understood that parenting was a lot of work and that they would feel tired occasionally. One thing that neither

Carlos nor Maria understood, however, was just *how* much work parenting was and just *how* tired they would be all the time. They also did not count on having to give up activities that they enjoyed. When they had their first child, they continued to try to go out to nice restaurants and museums. They quickly found out how difficult those activities were with a child. So, Carlos and Maria changed their ideas about what parenting was: It wasn't just doing more because of the child; it was also doing less because of the child. Maria was also amazed to find out that being a mother meant being creative. She was continuously trying to come up with ways to get the children to do what she wanted them to do. Just telling them was not enough. Sometimes they would do just the opposite of what she wanted because they were trying to assert their independence. Initially, Maria dealt with these episodes of stubbornness by losing her temper. Even though she tried to be patient and wanted to be understanding, some days she could no longer stand the strain of being a mother and ended up snapping at the kids. After a while, she found that by making things into games, she could get her kids to cooperate more. By using this strategy, she lost her temper less frequently. She also understood that punishing a child or yelling at a child was also part of being a good parent. Children need to learn boundaries.

No doubt Carlos and Maria's ideas about parenting will continue to change with the growth of their newest family addition, but they now understand that good parenting means many changes.

Application Questions

Using Kelly's personal construct theory, analyze Maria's and Carlos's behavior by answering the following questions.

1. Explain how Kelly's theory could suggest that Maria is a scientist.

2. What seems to be one of Maria's and Carlos's important personal constructs? Explain the construct.

3. What did Kelly mean by the dichotomy corollary? Find an example of it in the case study.

4. What did Kelly mean by the individuality corollary? Find an example of it in the case study.

5. What did Kelly mean by the fragmentation corollary? Find an example of it in the case study.

6. What did Kelly mean by the commonality corollary? Find an example of it in the case study.

7. What does Kelly mean by a permeable construct? What does the experience corollary mean? What does the modulation corollary mean? Are Carlos's and Maria's constructs permeable? Give examples of the experience and modulation corollaries.

Theory Comparison Questions

1. Compare Kelly's concept of a construct to a schema.

2. Explain Maria's change in parenting style (e.g., her encouraging her children's cooperation by making requests into games after her requests were refused) using Bandura's concept of reciprocal determinism. How does Bandura's concept of reciprocal determinism compare with Kelly's theoretical concepts?

3. How could Skinner's radical behaviorism explain Maria's change in parenting style to encourage cooperation by her children? How does the focus of Skinner's theory differ from that of Kelly's?

Kelly

Case Study 20

Philip is a member of the clergy, a priest in the Roman Catholic Church, and has been for almost 25 years. His religion has been important to him ever since he was a young child. He grew up in an Irish Catholic family that was involved in the parish and said grace before each meal; they went to church every Sunday; and Philip was an altar boy. It seemed natural for him to become a priest: He was involved in his church; had a strong faith; and had an uncle who was a priest and a cousin who was a nun. His family looked highly on that occupation, and it seemed to be one of the most prestigious careers he could aspire to.

As he nears his 25th anniversary of becoming a priest, he reflects on the differences between members of the clergy and those who were not members of the clergy. He considers that clergy members have an incredibly important responsibility of guiding their followers spiritually. This responsibility weighs on him. Occasionally, he is envious of his parishioners who do not have this duty, but then he remembers how fortunate he is to be one of those God called to be a religious leader. It helps to discuss this concern with other clergy members who understand and experience this feeling of obligation as well. He also considers the things he has had to give up as a Roman Catholic priest. Priests are not allowed to marry and, indeed, even take a vow of chastity. It has been difficult for him to have never known the love of a woman and to never have been able to father his own children. Likewise, not having had sex was difficult, especially when he was younger. It was more difficult to keep his vow of chastity than it was to keep his vow of obedience to the Bishop. Now that he is getting older, that is not as much a concern. He comforts himself with the thoughts of the close friendships he has formed, the children of friends he has been able to enjoy, and the knowledge that he is doing God's will.

Other religious leaders from other religions, however, do not believe that being a clergy member means giving up family life or sex. These clergy members are not required to take the vows of chastity that Philip did. Philip is aware of these differences and still believes that his requirements are the best way to serve God. Philip is also aware of a number of differences in the clergy within the Roman Catholic religion. In the last decade, a number of priests and nuns have voiced opinions about changes that they believe should be made within the church. An example of this is the notion that the Catholic Church should allow women to become priests. Only men have been allowed to join the priesthood because of the belief that all 12 of Jesus Christ's apostles were men and because of the belief that the priest is the presence of Christ among the people and only a man can represent Christ because Jesus was male. Today, these reformers believe that women should also be allowed to become priests because of theological arguments and evidence that supports the idea that some of Jesus' disciples were female and because of the Women's Movement. For example, some feminist theological research suggests that women were early Church missionaries and apostles. Reformers believe that changes like these will modernize the Church by relying on earlier church traditions and encourage people to come back to the Roman Catholic religion. Philip disagrees with them. He is not a reformer and does not understand the reasoning these people have. How could these church leaders revoke what they had been taught and what they swore to execute?

Philip also considers other difficulties he has encountered in his religious career. One of the most disconcerting experiences he has had to adjust to was how people reacted to him when they learned that he was a priest. Either people avoided him when they saw his collar, or if they interacted with him, they were cautious about what they said. They were careful not to swear or say things that they thought would offend him. They were not themselves. He was aware of the change in people's behavior that he evoked. This made forming relationships outside the religious order difficult, and it made him uncomfortable.

Sometimes he would be invited over to parishioners' houses for dinner. He would enjoy talking to the smaller children who would ask questions like, "Do you wear your collar when you go swimming?" He found that talking to the children, answering their questions at the child's level, would often put him more at ease with the parents. Philip liked to be able to take breaks from being a "holy man" and occasionally feel like one of a family.

Application Questions

Using Kelly's personal construct theory, analyze Philip's behavior by answering the following questions.

1. What is the organization of Philip's construct of clergy?
2. What are the two poles of Philip's clergy construct? What corollary does this apply to?
3. How is Philip's clergy construct the same as other people's? What corollary does this apply to?
4. How is Philip's clergy construct different than other people's? What corollary does this apply to?
5. Does Philip's clergy construct appear to be permeable? Why or why not?
6. What is the sociality corollary? Find an example of it in the case study.

Theory Comparison Questions

1. How does Kelly's individuality corollary compare with Adler's concept of subjective perceptions?

2. Use Bandura's concept of self-regulation to explain Philip's maintaining his traditional religious beliefs, even when presented with reformist views. How does Bandura's concept of self-regulation compare with Kelly's modulation corollary?

Skinner

Case Study 21

Yolanda had always been an excellent student. In grade school, she always earned A's and B's, and the teachers always spoke highly of her during parent-teacher conferences. When her parents came home from these conferences, they often would repeat the positive remarks they had heard to her. She also excelled academically in high school even when she took advanced courses. She took algebra when she was in eighth grade, college algebra as a junior, and calculus as a senior. She also took physics and advanced biology in the later part of high school. She was on the honor roll each semester, achieving an average of over 90% each time. Again, teachers commented positively about her. The positive remarks and superior grades made her feel good about herself and boosted her self-esteem. At the end of high school, she was valedictorian.

Understandably, Yolanda was college-bound. She majored in psychology and again showed outstanding academic aptitude. Initially, Yolanda worked hard and earned excellent grades, but she was attending a large state university and the personal attention she was used to getting for her superior academic performance was not as readily forthcoming as it had been in grade school or high school. She no longer received trophies or certificates for doing well in her classes and, because most of her courses took place in large lecture halls that she attended with about 300 other students, her professors did not know who she was, let alone that she was one of the top students in the class. By her second semester, Yolanda's grades began to falter, and her GPA for the second semester turned out to be 2.01, a drop from her first semester GPA of 3.5. By the end of her third semester, Yolanda was on probation. She decided to drop out of college and try working in the "real world" for a while.

Yolanda waited on tables for the next year and took stock of her life. She did not really enjoy her job. She did not make as much money as she would have liked and was tired of rude and inconsiderate customers. She felt as though she could do more, and she felt embarrassed when she told old friends from high school that she was no longer attending college. She felt as though they were looking down on her. She also felt as though she had disappointed her parents. They had encouraged Yolanda to achieve, partly for her benefit but, because of discrimination they had faced during the 1950s and 1960s, partly to demonstrate to the world that African Americans could achieve as much as others. She then decided to try college again.

She applied to a smaller college close to home and was pleased to find that she was not a number there but, rather, a person to whom professors talked. She majored again in psychology, got to know her professors, and studied hard. She did well in her courses, achieving a 3.6 GPA her first semester back in school. She soon became known within the Psychology Department as a rising star. Her professors talked to her, listened to her ideas and questions, and guided her toward graduate school. Her advisor suggested that she conduct some research if she was interested in attending graduate school because competition for graduate studies in psychology is fierce. One needed to stand out from other good students to be accepted into a program. She began a research project the second semester of her junior year and completed it the first semester of her senior year. Under the guidance of her research advisor, she submitted her research findings to the Eastern Psychological Association, and it was accepted as a poster presentation.

Yolanda's superior college grades (she ended up with a 3.8 GPA), her good Graduate Record Exam scores, and her research presentation helped her to be accepted into a clinical psychology graduate program at a prestigious university. There, she worked closely with a number of advisors and eventually earned her Ph.D. She now works as a psychology professor at a smaller undergraduate college.

Application Questions

Using Skinner's radical behaviorism theory, analyze Yolanda's behavior by answering the following questions.

1. What motivates our behavior, according to Skinner's theory? Is it internally or externally motivated?
2. How could Yolanda's early success in school be explained by radical behaviorism?
3. How could radical behaviorism explain Yolanda's dropping out of college?
4. How could Skinner's theory explain Yolanda's decision to go back to college?
5. How could Skinner's theory explain Yolanda's success in college the second time and in graduate school?

Theory Comparison Questions

1. Use another theory, besides Skinner's, to explain Yolanda's academic success.
2. How could Adler's theory explain Yolanda's success? How does the focus of Adler's theory differ from that of Skinner's theory?
3. Use Bandura's concept of self-regulation to explain Yolanda's progression through her career.

Skinner

Case Study 22

It is Saturday night, and Colleen is sitting in her dorm room alone, fixing her nails, listening to music, and wondering what is happening to her. She is an 18-year-old college freshman from Mississippi attending a university in the Northeast and is having some trouble adjusting to college life. It seems to her as though people "up north" value completely different behavior than do those she grew up with in the South, and she is no longer as popular and as respected as she was back home. She is confused and depressed.

Colleen grew up in a family that had a strong southern heritage. Both her mother and her father were born in Mississippi, and their ancestors could be traced back to the Civil War. In fact, both families could boast that their ancestors had actually fought in the Civil War. This heritage was instilled in Colleen, who was also proud to be a Southerner and to have such a distinguished ancestry. As a child, Colleen would hear the stories of her relatives' past from not only her parents, but also from her grandparents. She could tell that they were proud of their lineage, and they were always pleased when someone expressed interest in their stories. When Colleen showed such interest, they showed their pleasure with a smile or hug and kiss. Sometimes they remarked what a good girl she was. As a teenager, Colleen was elected to the prestigious organization called the Daughters of the Confederacy, an organization in which she could socialize with influential others. To be elected to this organization, one had to be able to trace back one's ancestors to the Civil War.

Colleen always seemed to be very interested in social events. She often helped to organize them in high school, and it was crucial to her that the "right people" were at the "right parties" or "events." As a cheerleader, she organized such events as class rallies and bonfires, and she hosted her own pre-prom party. Colleen was always popular in high school because of these events. She was the person who knew everything about everyone, and others were always interested in finding out the latest gossip from her.

Her mother let Colleen know how proud she was of Colleen's ability to organize these social events and about her popularity, unlike Colleen's older sister, Kaye. Their mother often hosted social events herself and prided herself on her own abilities as a hostess. Kaye, on the other hand, seemed to be just the opposite of her mother and younger sister. Kaye was not interested in organizing social events, becoming a member of the Daughters of the Confederacy, or her heritage, and seemed to de-emphasize it. Whereas Kaye worked hard to de-emphasize her Southern accent, Colleen emphasized hers such that she actually had a stronger accent than either of her parents. Whereas Colleen was very interested in clothes and makeup, Kaye was not interested in them at all and often looked more masculine, even in body type. Colleen was very slight and avoided physical activity other than her cheerleading; Kaye had a more athletic build and was on the track team. Both sisters were smart, however. But whereas Kaye had no problems with others knowing she did well in school, Colleen preferred to not let on that she did well and would sometimes pretend to not know something when she did know. She rarely spoke up in class and was often referred to as a perfect student by her teachers. Kaye, on the other hand, was very vocal and sometimes challenged her teachers. Their mother preferred Colleen to Kaye because Colleen was more similar to their mother. Kaye knew that her mother disapproved of her behavior but did not care.

Now it seems to Colleen that everyone at college is more like her sister than like her mother. The other students have remarked about Colleen's southern accent and have suggested she try to tame it because it makes her sound stupid. The other students have not enjoyed her gossiping because they believe she is betraying confidences. Even the way she dresses does not fit in with the other students. She wears dresses or designer jeans and make-up all the time; her roommates wear black jeans and tee shirts and no make-up. Some of the other women even have their noses pierced and tattoos on their bodies. Colleen's grades are hurting too. Many of her professors require class participation and part of students' grades are determined by that, but Colleen is reluctant to talk in class, thinking that it seems like showing off. Her fellow students, who value intelligence, are also beginning to wonder if Colleen is stupid because she is still hiding what she knows.

Colleen wishes she had never left the South. She had followed her boyfriend to college in the North, and he left her for another woman he met in one of his classes only four weeks into the semester. Now she has no female friends and even the men in her classes are not interested in her. At home, boys continually asked her out; now the men she is interested in are not interested in her! She is wondering whether she should finish the semester or whether she should just go back home now and transfer to a Southern college.

Application Questions

Using Skinner's radical behaviorism theory, analyze Colleen's behavior by answering the following questions.

1. According to Skinnerian theory, why did Colleen express so much interest in her heritage and in social events?

2. What reinforced Colleen's interests in her heritage and in social events, according to Skinner's theory? Give specific examples. Are they primary or secondary reinforcers? Why?

3. Which of Colleen's behaviors are not rewarded anymore in college? What term in radical behaviorism could be used to describe this?

4. According to radical behaviorism, why would Colleen be experiencing depression?

5. According to Skinner's theory, why would Colleen transfer out of college?

Theory Comparison Questions

1. How does Bandura's concept of reinforcement compare with Skinner's?

2. Apply Kelly's personal construct theory to Colleen's college experiences. What appear to be her superordinate constructs? Are her constructs permeable?

3. Use Erikson's concepts of identity versus role confusion and intimacy versus isolation to explain Colleen's college experiences. How does the focus of Erikson's theory compare with that of Skinner's theory?

Bandura

Case Study 23

Drew has returned to Albany, New York, for the memorial service of his dear friend Ruth. He lived with Ruth for three years while he was attending school in Albany. He was 23 at the time he moved in; Ruth was 73. His cousin, who attended the same church as Ruth, introduced the two of them because Ruth occasionally rented out two of her rooms to boarders. As a close friend of Ruth's, Drew is to deliver a eulogy in her honor. As he sits down to write his tribute, he contemplates Ruth's life, which had been fairly remarkable.

Ruth, a third child in a family with six children, lost her sight when she was just 5 years old. At a time before antibiotics, she had contracted meningitis and had to stay in bed for a week with a high fever. The doctor did not think she would survive. She did survive; unfortunately, however, she lost her sight. She was determined, though, to live her life as a "normal" child—that is, one who could see. This determination was sometimes taken too far, and Drew still smiles as he recalls some of the stories Ruth told about her childhood. She would roller skate with her friends and even learned to ride a bike! On at least one occasion, Ruth walked on top of a fence—without assistance. A neighbor stopped her before she got to the end of the fence and fell off. Ruth wanted to go to school like her brothers and sisters but at that time, visually impaired children did not attend school with the other children. Ruth made her brothers and sisters do their homework aloud so she could learn.

Ruth only expressed feeling sorry for herself once. She was frustrated with her inability to do something that seeing people could do easily. When she expressed her frustration, her mother started to cry. Noticing how upset her mother was about Ruth's distress, Ruth never again expressed sorrow at her loss of sight.

When Ruth was 10 or 11, she took the train from Jamestown to Batavia to attend the Batavia School for the Blind. There she learned survival skills, including Braille, typing, and ways that visually impaired people could get along in a world full of people with sight. For example, she learned to put a piece of tape under the salt shaker so that it could be distinguished from the pepper shaker; she learned to distinguish between dollar bills of varying amounts by putting paper clips on them.

As an adult, Ruth continued to be very independent. She could have had a guide dog when they began to be used but she felt that they took away her independence because they had to be cared for. She had a cane, but did not want to use it. She thought the cane made a person seem too obvious. And Ruth did not want to be obvious. In fact, she was determined to behave in the same ways seeing people did. She sometimes did such a good job at it that others thought she could see. Once, when she was at the dentist's, he held out an instrument for her to take; Ruth, of course, could not see it and so did not take it. He asked her why she wouldn't take the instrument and was surprised when she replied that she did not see. He had had no idea about her visual impairment. Ruth was quite proud of that story. More than anything, she did not want to stand out from others, especially from those who could see.

Ruth felt that visually impaired people were discriminated against in society and were sometimes perceived as being a burden. They were also sometimes viewed as having other disabilities besides blindness. For example, strangers would sometimes talk loudly to her even though there was nothing wrong with her hearing. When she was out at a restaurant with someone, the server would sometimes ask her friend what Ruth wanted to eat, as though she was mentally incapacitated as well. So, Ruth did her best to behave as seeing people did.

As an adult, Ruth was a home teacher for the blind until she met Kevin, who became her husband. They met at a social function for visually impaired people; Kevin was also visually impaired, although not totally blind like Ruth. After they were married, Ruth helped her husband manage his newspaper/candy stand, which was located in a factory in Buffalo. This was a state job geared specifically for the visually impaired, and they sold assorted sundries. Later they moved to Albany and managed a similar stand at the state capital. This was a very interesting enterprise because Kevin and Ruth were able to meet and get to know many politicians. They knew all the assemblymen and all the governors, and likewise, the politicians knew them. Ruth's favorite governor was Nelson Rockefeller. She thought he was very vivacious.

Kevin and Ruth retired after a number of years and, as is fairly typical, her husband preceded Ruth in death. She lived alone for a number of years until some friends encouraged her to help Drew by taking him in as a boarder. Ruth initially did not want Drew as a boarder. It had been years since she had had a boarder, and she wasn't sure she wanted to adjust to a new one. Conversely, it was Drew who had some trouble adjusting to living with Ruth. Her house was always neat as a pin, and she always had a place for everything. She had to. Because she could not see, she had to keep things where they belonged so that she could find them, and she had to keep the house clean so that she would not trip and fall on something that was left out. Drew was fairly disorganized and sloppy. Eventually he adjusted to Ruth's lifestyle, and they became good friends. Drew thought that one of the reasons why Ruth's mind remained so sharp, even until her death, was because she continuously was using her mind because she could not rely on her sight. Eventually, Drew married and moved away, but Ruth and he kept in touch with phone calls. In many ways, Ruth was a surrogate mother to Drew, and he knew he would certainly miss her.

Application Questions

Using Bandura's social cognitive theory, explain Ruth's personality by answering the following questions.

1. What does Bandura mean by reciprocal determinism? Find an example of it in the case and describe the interrelationships between the factors.

2. What does Bandura mean by self-regulation? Find an example of it in the case and describe it. Be sure to mention each of the stages of self-regulation involved in the example; that is what happens during the self-monitoring, self-evaluation, and self-reaction stages?

3. What processes are involved in self-regulation, and how do they apply in the example you just described? What are some of the external factors in self-regulation? Explain them using your example.

Theory Comparison Questions

1. What fortuitous event had a major impact on Ruth's life? What does Bandura's theory say about such events? How does this aspect of his theory differ from other personality theories?

2. Apply Adler's theory to Ruth's life. Specifically, discuss her striving for success and style of life. Compare Adler's theory with Bandura's.

3. Apply Erikson's theory to Ruth's life. Which stages appear to have been completed successfully? Which have not? Explain. Compare Erikson's theory with Bandura's.

Bandura
Case Study 24

Evonne is sitting at the table with a cup of tea. She has just tucked her kids into bed, and this is the first time she has had to herself all day. She wonders if her decision to stay at home was the right one. Her days as a mother and homemaker are certainly more exhausting than her days were when she worked as an accountant at a physician's office. She is continuously cleaning the house or meeting the demands of her children. It is amazing how much mess such little people can make. It seems as though they drop what they have in their hands anywhere they stand. Her son, Joe, for example, comes in from school, takes off his coat, and drops it, along with his backpack, on the kitchen floor in front of the door he came in. He places his hat and mittens on the kitchen cupboard located next to the door he just walked through. Sometimes, when he is excited to show his mother something he made at school, Joe dumps his backpack out onto the floor to find it. When he is through, he leaves the rest of the stuff on the floor and runs off to play with his sister. Although Evonne keeps reminding Joe to pick up his stuff and put it where it belongs, he does not seem to remember to do it from one day to the next. Not surprisingly, Joe often cannot find the things he needs because he did not put them in their place when he was through with them. Actually, he is a lot like his father, Blake, in that way. Blake is always losing and looking for things, especially his wallet because he does not put his belongings in the right place either. Now that Evonne thought about it, Blake seemed to drop things wherever he was standing also, and although Evonne scolded Joe for it, she rarely complained to Blake about his sloppiness—at least not in front of the children.

As Evonne thought about this similarity between Blake and Joe, she also noticed other similarities in their behavior. Lately, Joe has been trying to deflect punishment for wrong doing by charming his way out of it. It struck Evonne that this was similar to Blake's behavior when he made her angry: He would often try to alleviate the mood and avoid an argument by complimenting her or joking about his or her behavior that they were discussing. Sometimes it worked, and she laughed, hugged, and kissed her husband; sometimes it didn't work. Now Joe was doing the same thing. When he said something to her that he shouldn't have, for example, Joe would laugh and give her a big smile and bat his eyelashes at her. Sometimes she couldn't help but laugh back.

At other times, Joe would just try to make his mother laugh by telling jokes. He loved to see her smile. Most of the time, his jokes were pretty bad, but every once in a while he would tell a good one, and Evonne would chuckle. Recently, Joe has been asking whether his jokes were good or not. He is disappointed when his mother tells him that his joke is not one of his best and ecstatic when she says it is good.

Joe does other things that his father does as well. For example, Joe calls out, "Special night!" when he wants to just have fun that evening and watch a video and eat popcorn. Blake would sometimes call out that phrase or something similar when he wanted to have fun with his family and when there would be no work that day. Joe even wants a "libation"—a fun drink such as a soda—on these occasions, and Evonne knows that Joe picked up that term from Blake, who also enjoyed grown-up "libations." Joe, for example drinks root beer when his father has a beer.

Joe seems to have his father's self-confidence also. For example, Joe, at the age of 8, is a little computer whiz. He had seen his father working on their home computer and his peers working on the computers at day care when he was younger. He had had no qualms about sitting down at the monitor and trying to play various games. He became frustrated at times, but Blake encouraged him. Joe eventually learned how to use the mouse and became quite proficient at computerized tasks. This amazed Evonne because, although she now knows how to use the computer, she at first was terribly intimidated by computers and thought that she would never be able to understand them. Joe had had no such reservations. Yes, there really were quite a few similarities between Joe and Blake. The phrase "like father, like son," comes to Evonne's mind.

Application Questions

Using Bandura's social cognitive theory, explain the similarities between Joe's and Blake's personalities by answering the following questions.

1. How could Bandura's social cognitive theory explain the similarity between Joe's and Blake's behaviors?

2. List some examples of observational learning from the case.

3. What factors determine whether or not we will learn from a model, according to Bandura's theory? Choose one example of behavior learned through modeling from the case and explain the influence of these factors.

4. Find an example of self-regulation that Joe engages in. Explain it.

5. How would Bandura's theory explain Joe's confidence in using computers and his competence in using them?

Theory Comparison Questions

1. Use Skinner's radical behaviorism to explain Joe's computer competence. How does Skinner's explanation compare with Bandura's explanation?

2. What behavioral techniques could Evonne use to encourage Blake and Joe to become neater? Explain.

3. Apply Kelly's personal construct theory to Blake's and Joe's behaviors. Specifically, use the sociality corollary to explain Joe manipulating his mother (by giving her cute looks) to avoid punishment; use the commonality corollary to explain Joe's and Blake's sloppiness. Compare Kelly's experience corollary with Bandura's concept of modeling.

Trait Theories
Case Study 25

Walter is a 55-year-old minister of a conservative Southern Baptist Church. His congregation is small; less than 100 people attend his church, and most of those people are 50 years or older. He is concerned that his church is not growing because younger people are not joining and is afraid that with time it will actually die out.

Walter has always been religious, having been raised in a religious family. When he was a teenager, he received a "calling," which he describes as God telling him to become a minister. To fulfill God's will, Walter enrolled at a Seminary but flunked out his first semester. He was not dismayed, however, and believed that God was guiding him to the correct path to fulfill His will. Walter enrolled in a Bible School from which he subsequently graduated. After Bible School, Walter was eventually "called" to be interviewed at the small church that he now leads.

His choice of profession is an appropriate one because Walter has a handicap that would make other, more physical, types of work difficult. Walter was born with one leg shorter than the other, and he limps quite dramatically. Walter believes that his Church is just one of the many examples of God providing for him. To supplement his income as a minister, Walter also sorts small packages for a delivery service. He really does not worry too much about money because he has faith in God taking care of his needs. Occasionally, he wishes for more material possessions, but Walter also knows that he should not be concerned with such worldly goods. He struggles between worldly wants and spiritual needs.

His congregation trusts and admires Walter. Walter is good at what he does and confident of his abilities as a minister. He is a motivational speaker with a booming voice who delivers inspirational sermons. He moves slowly and precisely because of his handicap, and these characteristics seem to have permeated the rest of his personality. He is a cautious man—he had to be cautious in his movements—and he thinks long and hard before making decisions. His decisions, like his movements, are meticulously made. He carries himself with authority.

Walter tries to fulfill not only his spiritual needs but those of his family and his congregation as well. He wonders what his responsibility is to others who are not part of his flock. He believes that although other people attend church, they will not be able to enter heaven at the Time of Redemption because they are members of the wrong church and do not have the correct beliefs. Should he tell them this? Or should he concentrate on his own following? He believes the end of the world will come soon. To him, the societal changes occurring are signs of the forthcoming end. These changes are disturbing to him. He believes they are signs of immorality and that God is most displeased with these changes.

Walter met his wife, Lillian, at the church that he heads. He was pleased that she agreed to marry him. He thought that no one would want to marry him because of his handicap. Lillian was religious, and conservative as well, so Walter and Lillian made a good match. Lillian was especially pleased to serve God by becoming a minister's wife and had no qualms about agreeing to be submissive to her husband because the Bible indicated that it was the right thing to do. She certainly was submissive to Walter. Walter was, without a doubt, the head of the family. Both Lillian and their children obeyed anything he said. His every whim was granted. That is, until recently. With his children grown and with children of their own, there has been some strife about such things as where Sunday dinner would be held or whose house Christmas should be at. These events were always held at Walter's house, but now his children want them at their houses. As head of the household, Walter believes that there should be no discussion; they should be at his house. For Walter, this is yet another example of the moral decay of society that indicates the coming of the Lord.

Application Questions

Using Cattell's trait theory approach, describe Walter's personality by answering the following questions.

1. If one considers Walter's attendance at Seminary and Bible School as attitudes (according to Cattell's definition), what would be some of the sems or sentiments that motivated those behaviors? Why? Explain.

2. What would be some of the ergs that motivated Walter's choice of profession, according to Cattell's theory? Why? Explain.

3. What would be some of the ergs that motivated Walter's marriage and the formation of his family, according to Cattell's trait approach? Why? Explain.

4. List some of Cattell's 16 source traits that Walter might score high on. Which might he score lower on? Why? Explain.

5. Describe Walter's temperament traits, according to Cattell's trait approach.

6. Describe Walter's ability traits, according to Cattell's theory.

Theory Comparison Questions

1. How do Fromm's character orientations compare with the traits discussed by other theorists?

2. Use Jung's personality types to describe Walter's personality. Would he be considered an introvert or an extrovert? What would his superior functions be? How do Jung's types compare with the traits discussed by other theorists?

3. Apply Adler's theory to Walter's behavior. How does Adler's style of life compare with the traits discussed by other personality theorists?

Trait Theories
Case Study 26

Eric is a beginning assistant professor of meteorology in a medium-sized university in the Midwest. Sometimes he wonders how he got this far. During graduate school, he always thought that if he were going to be successful it would have to be because of his master's thesis or his dissertation or the articles he had written. He is fairly unattractive physically and has always been painfully aware of that fact. Likewise, he understands that his social skills are not the best. And so he did not believe that he would be able to obtain any type of job where he needed to interact with people in person. He assumed that he would be rejected at the interview stage and believed that his research and writing skills would have to get him a job.

Eric certainly was a misfit as a graduate student. He was the lone Jewish student in the Department of Meteorology and was quite aware of that. Indeed, he often reminded others of it by bringing it to their attention with reminders of upcoming Jewish holidays like Yom Kippur. He was very proud of his Jewish heritage—it was actually one of his defining characteristics—and his concern about increasing the awareness of others about the Jewish culture was certainly admirable. However, it was offset by his paranoia. He frequently felt persecuted because of his Jewishness. Any slight, real or imagined, was considered anti-Semitism. Some of these offenses, which we all experience at one time or another, were actually because of other characteristics besides his Jewishness.* For example, as a graduate student, he initially was not asked to be a teaching assistant because of his lack of social skills. The professors in his department did not believe that he could adequately fulfill the duties of the job. Eric, however, believed that he had been discriminated against because of his ethnic background.

He was an extremely precise researcher. His dissertation was based on a study of one storm that lasted five days. He spent two years studying the storm and another year writing up his analysis. Although it was very specific, it was an excellent piece of research, and he was able to publish it in a national journal.

---

*Author's note: This does not imply that there is no discrimination against Jews or other social groups in the real world.

Likewise, he was very exacting when he determined his forecast for a forecasting game the meteorology students played every week. The graduate students would determine their forecasts for a period of five days, and the student who was most accurate won the contest. Eric spent a lot of time determining his prediction, but even with this frivolous activity, Eric would show some paranoia. He was concerned that the other students would use his forecast as a basis for theirs and improve on it, thereby winning the contest. Therefore, Eric was very secretive about his forecast and was among the last to post his predictions, even if he had completed them much earlier.

Eric's meticulous nature also showed itself in his sole social outlet outside of work: his fantasy baseball league. At the time he played this type of game, they were played through the mail; today they are played on computers over the Internet. In this league, players play baseball seasons with members managing the team and determining such characteristics of the game as batting lineup. Players in the league would send each other necessary information, and then the player who received the information would play the baseball game and relay the results to the other members of the fantasy league. This activity suited Eric well because he preferred not to interact with many other people. He rarely went out, and even though he was heterosexual, he went to great pains to avoid women. He was convinced that no woman would be interested in him because he was physically unattractive. In fact, one first year meteorology student, who was a woman and who was trying to get to know the other graduate students, introduced herself to him, and he responded, "I'm Eric, you don't want to know me."

Eric did make a few friends during the time he was in graduate school. They were mostly other misfits like him, but these relationships took a long time to develop. Eric did not trust anyone until he knew that person for a long time. And, there were many other graduate students that he did not like or did not trust. He certainly did not endear himself to many of the other graduate students with his self-deprecation and his persecution beliefs. But even other, more minor, behaviors alienated Eric from some of the other graduate students. For example, his office was located next to the department mailroom, so many people would go in and out. His office mate, being a friendly sort, would often greet and talk to the other people who stopped to pick up their mail. This irritated Eric, and he would frequently comment that he was "working here!" Likewise, he would complain to his office mate about playing his radio; it disturbed Eric's ability to concentrate.

Some of Eric's friends tried to get him to try other activities, but they were unsuccessful. He did not want to go to any museums, sporting events, or the theater. Eric preferred a simple, uncomplicated life. In many of his practices, he was very set in his ways. His clothing and his apartment were all utilitarian, and when something wore out, he simply replaced it with something similar. He did not have a true sense of style and really did not care whether his apartment or his outfits were aesthetically pleasing. In fact, his only piece of clothing that was frivolous or decorative was his Boston Red Sox baseball cap.

Application Questions

Using the trait theory approach, describe Eric's personality by answering the following questions.

1. Explain whether Eric would score high or low on each of McCrae's and Costa's Big Five dimensions and why you think so.

2. List Eric's traits according to Eysenck's theory. Explain why you chose them to describe Eric.

3. What would be some of the central dispositions of Eric, according to Allport's theory?

4. How are the traits of the previously mentioned theorists different? How are they the same?

Theory Comparison Questions

1. Compare Eysenck's conceptualization of introversion and extroversion to that of Jung.

2. Which of Horney's neurotic trends is Eric displaying? How do these trends compare with the traits of other personality theorists?

Evolutionary Psychology
Case Study 27

Latisha is lying on one of the tables in the emergency room thinking about how she ended up there. Jeremy, her husband, left her on the floor of their apartment in a huddle after beating her for almost a half hour. The beating itself didn't come as a surprise; she was used to Jeremy hitting her. He had been doing so for at least two years now. She saw the warning signs that he was about to "lose it" again. He had become increasingly critical over the last week. He complained about everything and blamed her for anything that went wrong or for anything he didn't like or that didn't live up to his standards. Yesterday, he complained about her making dinner too late and that he didn't like the chicken. He even told her that she should have known that he wouldn't have liked the meal that she prepared and that she was stupid for not knowing that. The day before, Jeremy expressed his dissatisfaction with the way that the laundry was done: He said his shirts were wrinkled even though she had ironed them, that his socks and underwear were not put in the drawer correctly, and that she was lazy for not doing these things the right way. The day before that, Latisha had asked Jeremy about a credit card bill that she had opened up. He became enraged that she looked at the bill and, more importantly, that she had asked him about why it was so large. He told her it was none of her business and to keep out of his affairs. The truth was that even though Latisha asked Jeremy about their finances, he didn't provide her with any information. Instead, he told her that she didn't understand money, so there was no reason for him to waste his time explaining it to her. In fact, Jeremy controlled their money completely. Even though Latisha worked part time as a bank teller, she did not keep her paycheck: she never even saw it. She just handed over her paycheck to Jeremy who then gave her a small stipend for running the house and buying groceries. This financial arrangement began when they were first married. Jeremy had gotten a computer program to keep track of their finances and insisted on using it, although Latisha was reluctant and had trouble understanding and using computers. She was puzzled about this software purchase because Jeremy knew she didn't like to use computers. Although she tried to understand the software program, she just couldn't, and Jeremy didn't try to explain any of it to her except late at night when she was tired and just wanted to go to bed. She finally gave up and let him handle the finances.

This time the precursor to the attack was her talking to another man at a party they had attended. Jeremy had always been the jealous type, even when they were dating but it seemed to have gotten worse since they were married. Jeremy had never wanted Latisha to meet his friends and discouraged her from having male friends of her own. He continuously accused her of watching other men and occasionally inferred that she was interested in having an affair. This evening Latisha had met an old college friend at the party and was reliving old times with him. She could immediately tell that something was wrong when she left the party with Jeremy. He was very cold to her as they left and in the car ride home. When they got home he accused her of flirting with the college friend and arranging for a rendezvous with him, and then he hit her. When she denied any sexual interest in her old friend, he became even more enraged and continued to hit and kick her until he finally left her on the floor when he stormed out of the house. Latisha knew that she was hurt and needed medical attention but couldn't drive herself to the hospital. She finally found enough energy to call a friend who came to pick her up and drive her to the emergency room.

As she lay in the emergency room, she also thought that she was lucky have a friend to drive her there. She had very few. She used to have a lot of friends before she was married, but now Jeremy insists on always knowing where she is and whom she is with. Moreover, he is very particular about who she is with. It seems as though, one by one, Jeremy has driven away her friends by being rude to them or by forbidding her to call and keep in contact with them. She even has very little contact with family members because Jeremy disapproves of them.

No, Latisha was not surprised about being beaten again; what surprised her was the severity of the beating this time and the threats against her life. The physician said it looks as though she has a couple of broken ribs, as well as a split lip, black eye, and assorted other bruises. Latisha has never felt this bad after a confrontation with Jeremy, nor has she been this injured before. At the beginning of the relationship, Jeremy never hit her but sometimes would push her or grab her and shake her. After they were married, however, he began to slap her. Now the physical assaults were more extensive, especially since their discussions about having children. Jeremy wanted Latisha to get pregnant; he wanted children. Latisha, on the other hand, wasn't sure she wanted to have children with Jeremy. She wasn't even sure that she wanted to stay married to Jeremy, although she hadn't told him that until this evening. When Jeremy was accusing Latisha of wanting to sleep with her old college friend, Latisha lost her temper and threatened to leave Jeremy if he did not stop being so jealous. That was when the physical abuse escalated, and he told her that if she tried to leave him, he would hunt her down and kill her. Latisha also wonders if maybe she should just get pregnant and give Jeremy the baby he wants. Latisha does actually want to have children sometime. It was one of the reasons she got married. She thought that Jeremy's job as a store manager would provide a steady and reliable income, something that needs to be considered if a couple decides to have children. She thinks that maybe this is as good a time as any; maybe a baby would help the relationship with Jeremy.

Application Questions

Use the evolutionary psychology perspective to examine Latisha's and Jeremy's behaviors by answering the following questions.

1. According to evolutionary psychology, why does Latisha want to have children? Why does Jeremy?

2. Explain why Latisha chose Jeremy as a spouse, according to evolutionary psychology.

3. Why does Jeremy control the family finances and not allow Latisha access to any information on them, according to evolutionary psychology?

4. How does evolutionary psychology explain Jeremy's jealousy?

5. How does evolutionary psychology explain Jeremy's insults toward Latisha?

6. How does evolutionary psychology explain Jeremy beating his wife?

Theory Comparison Questions

1. Which of Horney's neurotic trends does Jeremy display? How does the focus on Horney's theory compare with that of evolutionary psychology?

2. How could behaviorism explain Jeremy's violent behavior toward Latisha? What motivates behavior according to behaviorists? According to evolutionary psychologists? How do the behavioral motivations compare in these two theories?

3. According to Fromm's theory, which need would be met for Jeremy and Latisha by having a baby? How does this concept of fulfilling a need differ from what evolutionary psychologists would suggest as a reason for wanting to have children?

Evolutionary Psychology
Case Study 28

Dylan is on his third marriage, and that now appears to be on the rocks. His wife, Cassandra, just found out that he was having an affair with another woman. She had suspected this for some time, but her suspicions were confirmed when she got home before Dylan and listened to the messages on the answer machine. One of the messages was his girlfriend, confirming an assignation later that week. Usually Dylan was the first one home and listened to the messages; any messages meant for Cassandra were written down by Dylan and given to her. She thought he was just being considerate by taking down the information; instead, he was making sure she didn't find out about "the other woman." Today had been atypical, however. After putting in many long hours at her marketing job and finishing a project, her boss gave her the afternoon off. This rarely happened, and she was looking forward to fixing a nice meal and having a romantic evening with Dylan. Instead, it turned into a terrible argument ending with Cassandra throwing Dylan out of the house.

This isn't the first time Dylan's marriage ended because he was having an affair. Both of his other marriages ended in the same way. During his first marriage, Dylan had had multiple affairs. His ex-wife, Whitney, knew about the affairs but accepted them because she thought that a man like Dylan needed more than one woman to satisfy him. He had always been sexually promiscuous, in high school and college, so she reasoned that as long as he loved her, it didn't matter that there were other sexual partners. Dylan and Whitney had two children together, but then Dylan's time away from her became too extensive and obvious. After a while, she got tired of being the only one to care for the children, and she felt used, no longer loved. Rather, she felt that Dylan was no longer interested in her and just kept her around to care for the house and the children. So she filed for divorce.

Dylan married again and had another child with his second wife, Nicole. Nicole had no idea of Dylan's sexual past. He had explained his first divorce was due to irreconcilable differences, but then a friend told Nicole about Dylan having an affair, and she filed for divorce.

Besides this recurrent pattern of affairs and marriages, Dylan has another noticeably repetitive pattern of behavior: All his wives share an uncanny resemblance: they are all very attractive: of medium height, with a slender, athletic build and shiny, long, blond hair, and complexions that are just slightly tanned. Dylan is attractive also, with an athletic build. Most likely, some of these similarities stem from the fact that Dylan usually meets his prospective wives at the fitness club he belongs to. A typical first date usually involves a tennis match and dinner afterward. Other dates often include going out dancing at a club. Dylan is an avid dancer. Dylan doesn't lack female attention. He is attractive and it is well known among the members of the fitness club that he is quite wealthy, with a steady job as a vice president of a software manufacturing company.

Interestingly, although Dylan is quite sexually promiscuous, he rarely uses contraception. Even when his dates ask him to use condoms, he refuses because of the decreased sensation. He never asks his dates whether they are on any type of birth control, either. He believes that if his dates, or his wives, are concerned about not getting pregnant or not contracting a sexually transmitted disease, the responsibility for prevention is theirs. Even though Dylan has had three children with his previous wives and is unconcerned about birth control, he is an uninvolved father, who rarely spends time with his children.

Application Questions

Use the evolutionary psychology perspective to examine Dylan's behaviors by answering the following questions.

1. How could evolutionary psychology explain Dylan's promiscuity?

2. How could evolutionary psychology explain Dylan's sexual interest in women who all look the same—that is, blond, athletic, tanned, and so forth?

3. Why did all the women in the case study want to marry Dylan, according to evolutionary psychology?

4. How could evolutionary psychology explain why Dylan's first dates typically include a tennis match?

5. Why isn't Dylan interested in raising his own children, according to evolutionary psychology?

6. Why doesn't Dylan use birth control, according to evolutionary psychology?

7. What are some problems with the evolutionary psychology explanations noted here?

Theory Comparison Questions

1. Use Freud's theory to explain Dylan's promiscuity. How does the focus of Freud's theory differ from that of evolutionary psychology?

2. How could Erikson's concepts of isolation versus intimacy apply to Dylan's relationships with women? How do the motivations for behavior in evolutionary psychology and in Erikson's theory compare?

3. How could Adler's concept of social interest apply to Dylan's relationships?

SECTION 2

Additional Theory Comparison: Multiple Explanations for the Same Behavior

---

Case Study 1

Every time Sarah calls her mother Myra, the conversation is very similar. Myra essentially describes that she is in the midst of cleaning her house. Sarah is well acquainted with this behavior. Myra takes great pride in the appearance of her house and yard and loves it when someone compliments either. As a child, Sarah remembers Myra continuously cleaning on weekends when she was not working outside her home. She would clean the entire house room by room, making beds, dusting furniture and woodwork, shaking out rugs. The entire process took a day and a half. When the family was expecting company at the holidays, it was expected that the house would be cleaned twice, once during the regular weekly cleaning and once the day the company was visiting. When company visited, the living room furniture, which was normally covered with plastic, was uncovered, and the sheet that was laid down on the rug in the living room entrance was picked up and put away. The plastics and the sheet helped to maintain the furniture and rug far beyond the usual life span. This helped the family to save money.

Once a year, spring-cleaning took place. Everyone in the family, except Myra, dreaded this process. During this event, closets were cleaned out and washed. Hardwood floors were washed and waxed. Woodwork and rugs were washed. Furniture was polished. Curtains were washed and re-hung. All the dishes were taken out of the cupboards and washed, and the cupboards were also washed. Then everything was returned to its place. Everything had a place in Myra's house, and she frequently would become angry if there were too many things out of place. "Family conferences" would be called to discuss ways to help keep the house clean and how hard Myra worked at keeping the house clean while everyone else did so little. Actually, this was a common theme. Myra frequently portrayed herself as a martyr who did so much for others and asked so little for herself. She sees herself as continuously doing for others, when actually, she usually told others what to do.

The yard is also very tidy. The grass is beautifully trimmed and resembles a rug. It is often mowed, even though it does not appear to need it. The garden is well tended and it would be difficult to find a single weed in it. Once when a neighbor cut his grass without a catcher attached to the lawn mower and grass went flying into her garden, Myra threw a fit. After that, she did not talk to the neighbor for two years.

Now that Myra is retired, the cleaning continues. She always thought that it was her job to care for the house. She was always the one who oversaw the cleaning, although her children or her husband would help. Myra's mother always took care of their house and thought that it was the woman's responsibility to do so. Myra learned how to clean "correctly" from her mother. Both Myra's parents believed in physical punishment, and Myra and her brother were hit if they did something wrong. Myra was punished if she did not clean something thoroughly enough.

Myra made sure that her family saved money. Some of the activities that she engaged in to save money revolved around cleaning issues, such as the plastic and sheets used to save the furniture and rugs, but Myra saved money in other various ways as well. Sometimes Myra would wash and reuse aluminum foil. Leftovers were eaten even if they were unappetizing and no one felt like eating them. There was always a concern for money even though the family really was not poor, nor lacking in any of the essentials. This was so extreme that Myra would become agitated when someone borrowed 50 cents for a soda and did not return it. Myra would tell stories about relatives who would accept invitations at her house but did not return the invitations. The primary complaint about this was that she was tired of spending money on these occasions without ever getting something in return. In fact, Myra displayed a disturbing pattern of establishing relationships and then ending them by being rude. She would have an intense relationship with someone she had just started a friendship with, often having that person over for lavish meals and then complain about some aspect of that person's personality to Sarah. Myra would sometimes even criticize people to their faces, or she would just stop calling them. Often, these complaints revolved around the idea that Myra was superior to them in some way. For example, someone was too loud and Myra wasn't; Myra's house was cleaner; Myra's cooking was better; and so on. When these people no longer wanted to interact with her, Myra did not understand why.

The family very rarely spent money on anything except the necessities even though they were middle class and could afford it. Thus, they rarely engaged in activities such as going to the movies, and the children felt as though asking for a new toy was totally unreasonable.

Although Myra is still healthy and she could participate in a number of other productive activities, such as volunteer work, she does not, preferring to spend all her time and energy working on her house and yard. When she visits her grown children, she is dismayed by how messy their homes are, and she begins to clean them. She frequently complains about how other people don't know how to clean anymore and that her neighbors don't take care of their property as well as she does.

Application Questions

1. Does Myra display a certain personality type described by Freudian theory? What evidence is there for it? What caused it?

2. Why does Myra feel that cleaning the house is her responsibility? How would Jungian theory explain Myra adopting this traditional role?

3. How could radical behaviorism explain Myra's cleaning behavior? Find examples of reinforcement or punishment that might have influenced her cleaning behavior.

4. How could Bandura's social cognitive theory explain Myra's traditionally feminine cleaning behavior?

5. Which of Horney's needs motivate Myra? Which of Horney's neurotic trends does Myra demonstrate?

6. How could Horney's theory explain the discrepancy between Myra's idealized versus real image of herself?

7. How could Fromm's theory describe Myra's mechanism of interpersonal relatedness? What character type best describes Myra, according to his theory?

8. Explain whether Myra would score high or low on each of McCrae's and Costa's Big Five dimensions and why you think so.

Case Study 2

Peter has a dilemma. His work as a letter carrier is not fulfilling and is increasingly annoying and troublesome. He started this job just over three years ago. Peter has two bachelor's degrees and a master's degree. He retrained a number of times after he relocated to marry his wife who was an established professional. He moved to a rural town of only 4000 people where even general labor types of jobs are scarce. The nearest city, where he could attain professional work, is two hours away, and because Peter has a wife and three small children, he is reluctant to seek employment that far away. It would either mean a four-hour commute daily or living away from his family for part of the week. Peter has been trying to find more suitable work within the Post Office but has been unsuccessful because many of the supervisory jobs are attained through politics, rather than ability. Most recently, he was not promoted into a supervisory position at the post office in which he has been working because a co-worker was promoted instead. She deserved the position because she often filled in when the last supervisor was off work, but Peter could not help but feel resentful considering he interviewed very well, did his job well, and fulfilled the requirements of the position. In particular, he felt that his life experience before the post office was more valuable than additional years doing the same postal work. He is now considering quitting his job and staying home with his three young children.

As he considers this possibility, he realizes that his letter carrier job has actually been a strain on the family. Although he does bring in a pretty good income, his hours change weekly, and sometimes daily, and he is constantly on call, so often he gets called in to work in the early morning without any notice. He also is the person to fill in for the other letter carriers when they are on vacation or off sick. What this means is that he usually works when most people have time off—that is, Saturdays and summers. This is especially annoying to his wife who is a college history professor and has weekends and summers off, too. The first year he worked as a letter carrier, Peter figured out that his wife potentially has fifteen weeks off a year when she could occasionally travel or engage in other family activities. Peter was unable to take any time off at all with her because he was filling in for the other carriers. So one positive aspect of quitting his job is spending more time with his family. Peter feels as though he has been missing out on a lot concerning his children because he has been working so much. Certainly, staying home with the children would mean less day care for them and a smoother running home. Good dinners could be on the table, and the laundry could get done. His wife continuously complains about what a mess the house is and how much she has compromised so he could continue his job. On the other hand, quitting his job could make him feel like a failure. Although Peter is liberal and believes in equality between men and women, he still feels as though a good part of his identity comes from his job and how much money he earns. His wife does earn enough money to support their family comfortably: they could certainly pay their bills and afford to take an occasional vacation. Nevertheless, Peter is uncomfortable fulfilling the traditional female role of staying home and taking care of the kids and house. What will he tell someone he meets for the first time at a party and they ask him what he does for a living? After all, five years ago when he was unemployed and staying home with his firstborn, he took some ribbing from some of his friends for this activity. As he is considering what he should do, he is rethinking his ideas of what it means to be successful and what it means to be a man and a father.

Application Questions

1. How would Freudian theory explain Peter's behavior of wanting to be the breadwinner?

2. How could Jungian theory explain Peter's urge to quit his job and stay home with his family? How would Jung explain Peter's urge to continue working outside the home and earn money for his family?

3. How would Jung's concept of self-realization apply to this example?

4. How is Jung's concept of self-realization similar to Rogers's and Maslow's concepts of self-actualization? Is Peter showing signs of self-actualization according to Rogers? According to Maslow? Why or why not?

5. How could Kelly's personal construct theory explain Peter's behavior?

6. How could radical behaviorism explain Peter's behavior? How could reinforcement or punishment have influenced Peter's wanting to be the breadwinner? Peter's wanting to quit his job?

Case Study 3

Jason was born in eastern Colorado in the 1920s just before the Great Depression of 1929, the third of four brothers, to a stay-at-home mother and a father who could be considered a farmer and cowboy, both of German American descent. He describes his family as being poor during his childhood and recalls that their home was so small that in all except the worst weather, he was required to sleep on the front porch. Some nights it was so cold on the porch that he would wake up to a light dusting of snow on his blankets. Food was not always plentiful. He sometimes jokes that on a farm, selling crops came first; then came feeding the livestock; then came feeding the children. He was only half joking. Christmas, of course, was sparse for the children and so were new clothes. When Jason needed clothes as a small child, his mother would sew them, sometimes out of burlap bags.

Although the family was poor, they shared what they could with others who were less fortunate than they were. Jason recalls strangers stopping by their house during the Depression hoping for a meal. His mother would then add another cup of water to the soup pot and give a bowl to the stranger along with a piece of bread.

His family sold such vegetables as beets and squash from their produce truck. They also had cows, and it was Jason's and his brothers' job to sell and deliver milk from a milk truck. On a farm, children are expected to help with various chores. When Jason was assigned this particular task, he would combine the watery milk of some breeds of cows with the creamier milk of other breeds to make a good product and to ensure that none of his customers was cheated. He and his whole family took pride in their work.

He had a close relationship with his mother and nursed until he was three years old—until his two older brothers laughed at him. He stopped nursing because he did not want to be made fun of. He had a somewhat distant relationship with his father who was fairly uninvolved with his children. Jason's parents seemed to have a pretty good relationship though. They had met at a county fair when they were doing a show where they did a kind of square dancing with horses. Jason's mother's usual partner took sick, and she was paired with his (to be) father. Jason's parents married when his mother was only 16; his father was 28. They remained married for the rest of their lives. His mother had an eighth grade education; his father had a third grade education.

Jason was a teenager at the beginning of WWII and went to Denver with his friends to sign up with the army. Because he was not 18 yet, Jason had to get his parent's approval to join the army, which his father gave. Although he finished high school, Jason did not wait for his graduation ceremony. He was anxious to leave Colorado and to begin his own life. He had hopes of living a life that was more comfortable and sophisticated than the one he lived as a child. He reported for duty in the army immediately after completing his high school requirements. Jason was stationed on what could be considered the front lines of WWII, but he never had to battle the enemy. This was probably best considering that when he was a teenager, he went on a Sunday school hunting trip and used his father's gun to shoot his first—and last—rabbit. The animal was completely obliterated, and the experience disturbed Jason. Although Jason never states it, he probably joined the army because of peer pressure and because of the idea that "that was what real men did." It was important to Jason that he be perceived as a real man, and he perceived himself as rugged-looking even though he was actually fairly short and not very muscular.

After Jason got out of the military, he only went back to Colorado once, when his father was sick and dying of cancer. Jason spent some time in San Francisco with his friends and worked for an airline company washing airplanes. After a short time, Jason decided to enroll in the army to do another stint. After this second tour of duty, Jason left the army and attended college on the GI Bill. He majored in accounting, and although his academic record was not outstanding, he completed his bachelor's degree in just over three years by taking the maximum number of credits during the regular semester and by attending summer school. He supported himself with various temporary jobs like washing dishes.

While attending college, Jason met the woman who became his wife. They married after a brief courtship and had three children. Jason worked at Westinghouse in Buffalo to support his new wife, but a recession caused Jason to be laid off. Throughout his life, economics influenced Jason, and this time was no different. Jason again decided to enlist in the army. This time he could attend officer training school, which he did, because he had his college degree. The army would offer Jason some financial security.

Jason was not very involved in the raising of his children because of his position in the army. He worked long hours and often spent time on base after work at the officer's club to wind down.

During this time, Jason became increasingly distant from his family. He became more isolated from them and more involved in his work. Even his social life consisted primarily of going out with other men that he worked with, rather than going on family outings or dates with his wife. Even when he was with his family on weekends, Jason spent time with his friends when his wife was shopping at the grocery store. He became interested in art, music, and fine food and subscribed to as many as 10 magazines at a time on these topics. Jason became an increasingly cultured person, growing to appreciate the better things in life that he never had as a child. He encouraged his wife to become involved in the officer's wives club but she did not enjoy the experience. This emotional distance between Jason and his family, his wife in particular, came to a pinnacle when she decided to stop having sex with him.

Jason's wife and children later found out that he had been having homosexual relations with various men. When confronted, Jason claims to have been faithful to his wife. He believes that he never committed adultery because he did not have intercourse with another woman and claims he did not start his homosexual activities until after his wife "cut him off." Jason does not feel guilty about his extramarital affairs. Rather, he feels victimized because his wife wouldn't have sex with him, and he claims that the homosexual acts are nothing more than working out in the gym. His wife never divorced him, however. She died of cancer shortly after hearing about Jason's homosexuality.

Although Jason keeps in contact with his children, his relationships with them are distant. He has never remarried and continues to have homosexual experiences, but he does not have a regular partner. He expresses no regrets, but he does feel closer to his past than to his present or future. An example of this is that he attends many army reunions throughout the year but rarely visits his children or grandchildren.

Application Questions

1. How could Jason's homosexuality be explained from the Freudian perspective?

2. What was Jason's goal in life, according to Adlerian theory? Did he experience feelings of inferiority that influenced his life? How? How did he strive for success?

3. How could Horney's theory explain the difference in Jason's idealized versus real image of himself?

4. How would Sullivan's interpersonal personality theory explain Jason's lack of close relationships, especially with his wife and children?

5. According to Maslow, which needs in the hierarchy were met? Which were not?

6. Point out examples of Rogers's conditions of worth in Jason's life.

7. Point out examples of Skinner's behaviorism throughout Jason's life. Describe reinforcers and punishments and the specific behaviors they encouraged or discouraged, respectively.

8. Find an example of Bandura's fortuitous events that influenced Jason's behavior. How was his behavior influenced?

9. How could Kelly's theory explain the inconsistency between Jason's being homosexual and also wanting to be perceived as a "real man"?*

---

*Author's note: This does not imply that gay men are not real men.

Case Study 4

Derek was born in 1960 to an Irish American family that was about to become affluent. His mother was a nurse; his father was an "up and coming" lawyer who was already making six figures in the middle 1960s. Derek grew up in a beautiful house with his brother. His family also occasionally took in Derek's friends who were having hard times. For example, one friend stayed with their family for a year when the friend's family moved during his last year in high school and the friend did not want to move with his parents to another school.

Although Derek's family seemed to be living the American Dream, all was not well. His father was an alcoholic; the most likely cause of this was the pressure he was under at work and the long hours he spent there because of it. His drinking made him abusive and he would sometimes get into fights at bars. He beat his wife. Although Derek was not physically abused, he was scared for himself and his mother on these occasions. His father quit drinking when Derek was five or six years old.

Derek's father was an athlete: a boxer who was also a golfer. And, he encouraged athletics in his sons. Derek's older brother was tall, gangly, and not very coordinated. Their father was embarrassed by his older son's clumsiness and would comment that this boy couldn't possibly be his biological son. Derek heard these comments to his brother and was secretly afraid that he would hear similar comments about himself. Derek's father was very competitive, and Derek became that way, too. Derek wanted his father's approval and tried to get it by conforming to his father's wishes. Fortunately for Derek, playing sports came easy, but school initially did not.

Derek went to public school and was held back in the first grade. His parents decided that smaller classes might be better for him, so they sent him to an elite private school. He attended the private school for three years, and his academic performance improved. After three years, however, Derek wanted to attend school with his neighborhood friends, and he asked his parents to let him go back to the public school. His parents granted this request, and Derek earned good grades, mostly A's and B's, just as he did at the private school. Derek was also very popular in school. He was witty—the class clown—and everyone liked him, but his popularity and competitiveness in sports hid insecurity. He was concerned that he would not be able to live up to his father's standards.

In junior and senior high schools, Derek continued to excel academically, socially, and athletically. He did weight training in the seventh and eighth grades, before it was popular. He was captain of the football team at his large, city high school. He also played basketball but quit that sport because he realized that he would not get a lot of playing time. Derek liked attention and his antics in class along with his sports participation provided a lot of it. He received this attention not just from his peers but from his teachers as well. Derek could get away with things other kids could not. For example, he would often come to school late because he had stopped by a bakery on the way in. He would buy éclairs that were on sale and ask his teachers to store them for him. Then, at lunchtime, he would resell the éclairs at a profit. He got away with these schemes because his grades were good, he was an athlete, and he was charming. His superior record earned Derek acceptance into an exclusive college. Only one or two seniors from a typical class of 400 at his high school were accepted into Bowdoin College, and that year he was one of them.

Everything seemed to be going easily for Derek. His acceptance into Bowdoin was the next step of reaching his life's goal of becoming a lawyer like his father and working in his father's law firm. But Derek almost flunked out of college in his freshman year. Because everything came easily for him in grade school and high school, and because he was able to charm everyone then, he thought he could do the same in college. Being away from home for the first time allowed him his first taste of freedom, and Derek partied too much; he drank too much beer and smoked too much pot. He found himself failing his courses, especially freshman English. Derek approached the English professor and asked her what he could do to pull his grade up. She suggested extra credit, which he completed. The extra credit was not enough, however, and he failed the course. For once Derek could not charm himself out of trouble. His performances in his other courses were similar, and he was placed on academic probation. To make matters worse, his girlfriend, whom he started dating in high school, broke up with him. She told him he was becoming a jerk with all his partying.

Finding his life, and his dream of becoming a lawyer, crashing around him, Derek straightened up. He quit smoking pot, drank less, did extra academic work, and improved his writing. Eventually, he was able to convince his girlfriend to come back. He maintained superior academic performance for the rest of his college career and applied to get an exclusive internship with a state senator. Although he was a talented young student, he was most likely offered this internship through the influence of his father, who had political connections. With his education and internship completed, Derek applied to the law school his father graduated from. He was accepted but wondered whether his acceptance was the result of his own merit or whether his father helped to get him in. After law school, Derek applied for a position in his father's law firm, which he was offered. A few years later, Derek applied for a partnership in the firm, which he also earned.

Derek continued to have nagging doubts about whether his own performance earned his positions or whether his father helped him get his positions. He finally confronted his father, who replied that he had no influence on Derek's getting the initial position with the firm or getting the partnership, although he did help with the internship. His father stated that Derek went through the same hiring practices as everyone else and that he had excluded himself from the decision-making process when Derek was applying for his positions. Derek was finally convinced that he earned his partnership on his own.

While in law school, Derek married his high school sweetheart, and they had three children. He is a devoted family man who describes his children as "wonderful and beautiful." He plays with them often, and his wife sometimes describes him as her fourth child. He and his family live in a house next to the one he grew up in, and he enjoys attending functions at the school that he attended and that his children now attend. He is also active in the Congregational Church as an elder, a kind of church trustee.

Application Questions

1. Which of Erikson's stages did Derek successfully complete? Which were not completed? Why?

2. According to Adlerian theory, did Derek experience feelings of inferiority? Give some examples of it. How did these feelings influence his behavior?

3. Which of Fromm's existential needs are met for Derek? Why?

4. Which of Maslow's needs were fulfilled for Derek? Which were not? Did the fulfillment of these needs change at any time in Derek's life? Could Derek be perceived as self-actualized, according to Maslow's theory? Why or why not?

5. Find an example of Rogers's conditions of worth in the case study.

6. Find examples of Skinner's radical behaviorism in the case study. How did they influence Derek's behavior? Specify the reinforcers and/or punishments.

Case Study 5

Roger, at the age of 73, is in the process of examining his life. He is trying to determine whether he lived a life that was worthwhile. In the course of his examination, Roger contemplates the various stages of his life.

He was always a superior student, even as a child in grade school, especially in reading. In early grade school, however, he was not a popular child. He had very few friends. His concern with doing well in school did not endear him with his classmates who were less concerned with grades and more concerned with friendships and sports. He was also somewhat heavy, which hindered his athletic ability.

Roger experienced his pre-puberty growth spurt earlier than the other boys in his class did, so he was taller than the other boys during sixth, seventh, and eighth grades. This height increase slimmed Roger down; his weight stayed pretty much the same even though his height increased. Likewise, his height and strength now gave him an advantage in sports. In turn, excelling in sports made him popular in school. During high school, the other boys also grew, caught up, and even surpassed Roger's height. Because Roger experienced an early growth spurt, he also stopped growing sooner than the other boys did. In high school, he found himself to be below average in height. Nevertheless, Roger's increased contact with fellow students sharpened his social skills and his popularity continued throughout high school and college, where Roger continued to be a superior student and a very good athlete. Now his success in sports was due to skill and intelligence, rather than strength.

Although Roger could now easily make friends and maintained many same-sex friendships, he initially had less success at the love task, partly because he felt uncomfortable with being Jewish in a predominantly Christian area. Although he dated, he did not establish any long-term relationships with women until college. During college, he met Anita and eventually they were engaged. However, Anita later fell in love with another man and broke off the engagement. Although Roger tried to salvage the relationship, it was hopeless.

It was six years before Roger formed another long-term relationship and told another woman that he loved her. Jackie became his wife, and they were married for more than 40 years. Like all marriages, Jackie and Roger's occasionally had some difficult times, but Roger seemed to have found his soul mate in Jackie. They had three children: one boy and two girls.

During college, Roger chose his major and his career. In college, he majored in English because he had always loved to read. He then went on to graduate school where he earned a Ph.D. in English. After a few temporary instructor positions with colleges, he landed a tenure-track position as an assistant professor of English at a small teaching college where he stayed for the rest of his teaching career. He was especially glad to have gotten a permanent position because it was stressful not knowing whether he would have a job the following year. The time he spent job hunting took away from the time he wanted to do other things as a professor: improve lectures, advise students, publish. While at this long-term position, he eventually earned tenure and was promoted to associate, and then to full professor. His most rewarding experiences as a teacher included encouraging young writers. While teaching, he was also able to do some writing. He acquired a contract with a publisher to write fiction, and he published a number of science fiction novels. Writing really was his love because it allowed him to be creative. Many of his novels expressed a moral concern for the future that began with the birth of his first child. Although his novels have sold well and are respected, Roger continues to try to improve his writing and wishes he could do better.

Interestingly, some of his colleagues discouraged Roger from his writing. They did not publish and suggested that he should take it easy now that Roger was tenured and a full professor. Roger disagreed with this philosophy and, instead, believed that even full professors should continue to publish and grow as faculty members.

He retired from teaching five years ago but not from writing. Roger now travels with his wife, visiting his children and grandchildren, and seeing places he has not seen before. Along with his writing, the discovery of new places and the appreciation of the beauty in these new places keeps Roger satisfied.

Application Questions

1. Use Erikson's psychosocial stages of development (especially the fourth through the eighth) to analyze Roger's life.

2. Which dynamisms had to have been fused so Roger could establish a mature love relationship with his wife, Jackie, according to Sullivan?

3. How could Fromm's theory explain Roger's traveling and his visiting his children and grandchildren?

4. Find an example of how Roger's perceived self is different than his organismic self, according to Rogers's person-centered theory.

5. Roger had a different view than his colleagues did about how much work he should do after he was tenured and promoted to full professor. How could Kelly's theory explain this difference in views?

6. Using Cattell's concept of a dynamic lattice, describe the subsidiation chain involved in Roger studying English in college and graduate school. What are the ergs, sems, and attitudes involved?

TO THE OWNER OF THIS BOOK:

We hope that you have found *Personality Theories Workbook, Second Edition,* useful. So that this book can be improved in a future edition, would you take the time to complete this sheet and return it? Thank you.

School and address: _____

Department: _____

Instructor's name: _____

1. What I like most about this book is: _____

_____

_____

2. What I like least about this book is: _____

_____

_____

3. My general reaction to this book is: _____

_____

4. The name of the course in which I used this book is: _____

_____

5. Were all of the chapters of the book assigned for you to read? _____

   If not, which ones weren't? _____

6. In the space below, or on a separate sheet of paper, please write specific suggestions for improving this book and anything else you'd care to share about your experience in using the book.

_____

_____

_____

_____

_____

Optional:

Your name:_____   Date:_____

May Wadsworth quote you, either in promotion for *Personality Theories Workbook, Second Editon*, or in future publishing ventures?

Yes: _____   No:_____

Sincerely,

Donna Ashcraft

BUSINESS REPLY MAIL

FIRST CLASS   PERMIT NO. 358   PACIFIC GROVE, CA

POSTAGE WILL BE PAID BY ADDRESSEE

ATT   *Donna Ashcraft*_____

Wadsworth-Thomson Learning
511 Forest Lodge Road
Pacific Grove, CA   93950-9968